Reflections of the Susquehanna

Insights and Inspirations from the Susquehanna Valley

Larry L. Little

LOCAL HISTORY PRESS
an imprint of Sunbury Press, Inc.
Mechanicsburg, PA USA

LOCAL HISTORY PRESS
an imprint of Sunbury Press, Inc.
Mechanicsburg, PA USA

For information about special discounts for bulk purchases, please contact Sunbury Press Orders Dept. at (855) 338-8359 or orders@sunburypress.com.

To request one of our authors for speaking engagements or book signings, please contact Sunbury Press Publicity Dept. at publicity@sunburypress.com.

FIRST LOCAL HISTORY PRESS EDITION: Deember 2025

Set in Adobe Garamond Pro | Interior design by Crystal Devine | Cover by Lawrence Knorr | Edited by Debra Reynolds.

Publisher's Cataloging-in-Publication Data
Names: Little, Larry L., author.
Title: Reflections of the Susquehanna : insights and inspirations from the Susquehanna Valley / Larry L. Little.
Description: First trade paperback edition. | Mechanicsburg, PA : Local History Press, 2025.
Summary: The Susquehanna River is a unique environment, with many life lessons to be learned by simply observing its long lazy flow from New York to and including the Chesapeake Bay. All that is needed to learn those lessons is an open mind and an observing eye. Come with me and share my life lessons learned as I reflect on my youth and time on the river.
Identifiers: ISBN : 979-8-88819-361-7 (paperback).
Subjects: NATURE / General | NATURE / Ecology | NATURE / Ecosystems & Habitats / Rivers.

Designed in the USA
0 1 1 2 3 5 8 13 21 34 55

For the Love of Books!

I wish to dedicate this book to my two older brothers, Paul and Ronald, who encouraged me at an early age to get out and explore my world and especially to my best friend and co-conspirator on many of these adventures, Stephen Copp.

Table of Contents

Foreword

Our life cycle mirrors the life cycle of the Susquehanna River. The river's birth as small insignificant springs is as ours, crying in our cradle. The river gains its first tributaries, and tumbles down a remote mountain valley, churning and bubbling, just as we in our early years are rambunctious, and full of ourselves. As the river flows, it joins with other streams to become a small river, just as we, growing into our teens, our circle of friends growing. As it flows, the river joins other rivers such as the Juniata, coming to its maturity, broad, and sure of where it is going, just as we, as adults, settled with careers, are set on our path through life. Finally, our river comes to its culmination as it flows into the Chesapeake Bay, merging with the waters of the world, just as we, pass on into the great beyond, the cosmos.

PREFACE

What is It all About?

The view from back porch where the author grew up

Come with me and take in the *Reflections of the Susquehanna* from the back porch of the old house where I grew up, overlooking the river. It represents a simpler time and place where pressures and troubles are left behind. The porch stood elevated on the second floor of the house, abutting the kitchen. In this old house, the kitchen was always a center for family activities, from breakfast to dinner to playing board and card games in the evening. This was a time before the internet, cell phones, and personal computers, soon after the introduction of black and white television. It was a time when children played outside, when couples talked, and when families were truly families. The kitchen table was like the hub for the family, with members sitting at all sides. The kitchen was heated by an old wood and coal burning cookstove which kept it toasty warm in the wintertime. The cookstove was the place where boots and wet clothes were placed after venturing out into the snow, the boots placed on the floor and clothes hung on the back of chairs. Toasty warm in the winter, the kitchen was also cool in the summertime, as it was built against the historic bank of the Susquehanna River facing east.

If the kitchen was bustling, then the back porch was a retreat for relaxation and rejuvenation. The back porch was separated from the house in summer only by the old screen door. The screen door with its wood worn smooth by decades of opening and closing is the portal between bustle and relaxation. The porch is wide and deep with its wooden deck painted a battleship gray. The roof slants upwards to the back side of the house with supporting rafters. The porch roof was covered with tar paper. With no spouting, the rain dripped two stories to the ground below like a thousand miniature waterfalls. The harder it rained, the more impressive the waterfalls. There was a banister around the edge of the porch, running from roof pillar to pillar. The banister was painted a contrasting color, a forest green, also worn by years of the family gripping the rail to look at the view below.

Come with me now and visit this back porch from long ago. Looking from the banister, the view is of the wide backyard sloping to the shores of the Susquehanna River. This view is broken by several stately maple trees providing shade for picnics and games. Just to the left of the porch is a large lilac tree rising from below to the height of the porch roof. In spring, its prolific blooms and fragrance are not to be ignored; they grip you with both their beauty and aroma as you come onto the porch and close the screen door behind you. To the right of the porch in the side yard, beside the retaining wall that the kitchen is built against, stands a huge pink wild rose bush which has been there for as long as the family has lived in the house. It runs the length of the wall, some thirty feet wide, and is taller than the eight foot wall. As it blooms just once a year, it is magnificent with thousands of pink blossoms. This rose bush is the favorite nesting site of catbirds, and generations have returned to nest and raise their brood. In my mind, I can still hear the catlike call for which they are named. Next to the rose bush is an enormous forsythia bush, also blooming just once a year with brilliant golden hues.

The view from the porch railing changes as the seasons change. Spring with its freshness and sense of renewal melds into the warm lazy days of summer with picnics, games, and long evenings on the swing just talking and laughing. The fall season sneaks up on us and suddenly one day, the frosts and invigorating cooler days come into their own. Days of outings, raking, geese watching and all the joys of the harvest season, Thanksgiving in its true meaning. Winter comes on with the snow and ice, and a time of rest for the natural world as well as for us, as we watch the flakes fall. In winter, we make quick visits to the porch to fill the bird feeder and eat an icicle, then retreat to the warmth of the kitchen.

So, *Reflections of the Susquehanna* represents a study of youth, of family, of curiosity, and of human nature, in our interactions with each other and the natural world.

Sunrises and Early Morning on the River

It starts as a faint glow beyond the hills of the eastern horizon, far from the Susquehanna valley. As the minutes tick by, it takes on a crimson glow, glorifying the river scene below. As the shadows slowly fade, what can be seen is the myriad of boulders and surface grass patches that fill this broad, shallow river. As time passes and a warm midsummer day develops, the boy stirs from his warm bed, and opens one eye to peer out the ancient, distorted glass window of his bedroom towards the eastern sky. It is apparently not raining, so today he will spend outside. He is quickly dressed and flies down the two sets of stairs to the kitchen level, and more importantly the back door, leading to the well-worn elevated back porch. From here, he can canvas his realm. Below him the lush green lawn, fertilized annually by river floods, stretch to the Susquehanna River shore. He is quick to note that there is no appreciable change in the river's level, it is low and quiet, just as he likes it. As he watches, the sun peeks from beyond the eastern horizon in all its glory, allowing him a better view. Along the shore line, a muskrat swims past, its mouth stuffed with grasses to pad its den dug deep into the river shore. Then, further ashore, a feeding smallmouth bass swirls, taking an unlucky mayfly from the surface.

The bright sun is reflecting off the river, giving a glimmering effect to the underside of the big maple tree's crown. It is the end of the river's night shift, and the beginning of the day shift. During the night, the bass roamed the shallows, looking for unaware crayfish and minnows. Replacing them are the river's day shift. Just now a flock of swallows are doing gyrations, skimming the surface of the river, sipping water from the surface. Also coming to center stage are the dragonflies, mayflies, and caddis flies populating the air just above the river's surface. The caddis and mayflies are interested in mating, and continuing their species, while the dragonflies are looking for easy meals.

As the sun breaks free of the eastern hills, the river's surface remains still, allowing the full reflection of the sunrise, clouds, and eastern horizon, river-wide.

As the sun rises further, it raises a gentle breeze that stirs the river's surface to tiny ripples. As the low rising sun reflects off this ripple, it presents the viewer with the illusion of sparkling gems, beautiful to behold.

As the rising sun reaches the point where the changing angle ends the sparkling gem view, it instead presents the viewer with another image, one of a river very much alive, just waiting to be explored.

Under the Sea (River)

When you are a River Rat, it is important that you know as much about your home river as possible. For me, this started when I was about ten years old, full of myself, and adventuresome. My neighbor and best friend, Steve, and I discovered snorkeling one day when visiting the local five-and-ten-cent store. The owner had stocked snorkeling equipment: masks, breathing snorkels, and fins. I spent most of my life savings to buy a set, as did my friend. We were home for about ten minutes before to going to the Susquehanna to discover its deepest secrets. We stopped on the shore, sat down and put on the cheaply made fins (which snapped behind the ankle) and our masks, and waded out to our favorite swimming spot at that age, which we called "The Rock." There we pulled down our masks and dived under. It was a very different world. We swam down to the bottom and peered under the rock, to find multiple fish staring back at us in awe. It seems that when one is under water with the fishes, they are seen by those fish as just another of their kind, maybe a lot larger, and oddly shaped, but they were not frightened. My friend lost interest in snorkeling after that first summer, but I continued to dive for several years to follow.

There seemed to be a lot more aquatic grasses in the river in those days, with huge beds of eel grass on the bottom. I would dive at the edge of a bed and explore, finding numerous small minnows seeking shelter there. There were juvenile smallmouth bass, rock bass, sunfish, and others. I would capture some of these cuties in a tin can and take home in put them in an old goldfish bowl. They lived for a day or two, then went "belly up," because the bowl was not aerated. Those massive eelgrass beds were nurseries for many species of fish, as well as crayfish and numerous insect larvae.

This was the 1950s and trash pickup was not yet in vogue; everybody was on their own. I remember that my father, weekly, toted all our trash, including paper, cardboards, metal cans, and glass bottles, to the river shore and burned it. The combustibles burned, but the metal and glass were left behind for higher water levels to wash away. This was standard practice in those days, resulting in the river bottom being littered with everything from green bean cans, to catsup bottles, to every other non-burnable item. In addition, it was apparently the practice of the railroads to dump their used ties and worn rail plates (a plate, attached to the tie with spikes, that the rail nestled in) into the river, because old ties and plates were everywhere as well. It was not a pretty sight, but all this did provide home and shelter for crayfish and minnows. Over time the tin cans rusted away, the glass bottles were pulverized, and the ties rotted away; but it took years.

As I grew older, I dove into deeper water, to discover the worn backbones of the mountains that the Susquehanna had cut through in the millennia, worn down to these remainders on the bottom. As I state elsewhere in my musings, the Susquehanna River predates the mountains that it cuts through. In time, my scuba equipment wore out and the local store no longer carried the line, so my adventures turned to exploring the river's surface.

Snow Storms along the River

When I was a youth living in the old house on the shores of the Susquehanna River, I eagerly looked forward to the fierce snow storms that we had every winter. I would rise in the middle of the night and climb the stairs to the attic to peer out the window facing the streetlight just down the street. The snow came down in steady sheets, blown occasionally by strong breezes from the south. I would sit in the cold for an hour or more, mesmerized by the snow and the ghostly appearance it gave to the scene below. As I watched, I was also anticipating the fun that I would have the next morning because surely the schools would be closed. I could go out early to explore the fresh snow along the river shore. Although the snow came down steadily, the accumulation on the ground was not even and consistent. On the leeward side of the big maple a drift formed, created by the wind swirling around the tree. On the other hand, just in front of the tree, where the wind split to the sides, was less snow, the ground almost bare. Looking across an area of snow I could see tiny divots or projections, created by variations of the wind from spot to spot, adding character to the pallet of nature. It is the same way with us, with our souls and personalities. Life comes on in a rush as we develop, just as the snow storm rushes in and sweeps snow into drifts, eddies, divots, and projections. The drifts represent our strong points where our abilities are deep and strong. The eddies as at the tree represent our weak points where we need work and support. Lastly, the divots and projections represent our quirks that make us who we are.

Eddies

As a youth long ago, I had a wooden row boat that I used for fishing, swimming, and exploring the Susquehanna River. If you have observed the river, you have noticed that it is wide but shallow with many rocks, islands, and grass patches from shore to shore. The river picks it way through these obstacles with a strong flow, but immediately downstream from each is an eddy, where the river's current swirls to slack water or even upstream. I soon learned that it was easier rowing upstream if I picked my way from eddy to eddy, battling the current only when I needed to move to the next upstream eddy. This method was much easier than battling the direct flow to get to my destination. On the other hand, coming downstream, it behooved me to ride the current as much as possible. The point is that in life, as in rowing the river, sometimes it is better to avoid the currents, and sometimes it is better to go with the flow.

Susquehanna River Ospreys

When I was young, I spent much time in and on the Susquehanna River and loved to watch the ospreys hunting. They flew into the wind, slowly, at an altitude of several hundred feet. When they spotted an unaware fish on the river bottom, they would hover for an instant, fold their wings and dive for the water. Just above the water, they flared their wings, folded them back, and reached forward with their talons. Below the water they went, but when they arose, they were instantly in the air with their prey firmly in their grip. As they rose from the water, they would always turn the fish, head forward, with one talon behind the head and the other further back. The majestic birds then soared back to the Blue Mountain where their fledglings were hungry and waiting. The moral is, like the unaware fish, swimming along, we never know when the talons will strike, so live every day to the fullest.

Susquehanna River Shorelines

If you look at the shoreline of the Susquehanna River, you will notice that the shore itself is not lined with tall stout trees. The shore line is cloaked in short scrub trees such as alders and birches. This is because these trees bend under the weight of flood waters and ice floes. The stout trees, oaks, maples, and such, are further from shore beyond the main flow. If a maple should take sprout on the river shore, it may grow for some time, but eventually it will be uprooted and carried away. The moral is, depending on the circumstances of your life, sometimes it is better to bend under pressure to live another day.

On the Meaning of Life

Much has been written on the "meaning of life" from comedy skits by Monty Python to deep philosophical studies. This is my attempt to illustrate the meaning of life from a simple observational viewpoint.

Retreat from the daily pressures of life and take a slow walk along the river bank during springtime. Walk slowly and quietly, remember and contemplate what you see and hear. Do not prejudge anything. The Earth and all its environs have their own heartbeat, in a sense, the Earth itself is alive; be open to its call.

Near the shore, a female mudcat catfish has laid her eggs. Once laid, she swims away to feed and regain lost strength, but her male partner has stayed to guard the eggs from predators. The eggs have now hatched and a school of baby catfish feed in the shallows. Even now, the male mudcat continues to guard them. They carry his genes, and in a way, he will live on through these, his prodigy. At the first hint of danger, he gapes his mouth, and the entire school of young fish swims inside for safety. The male will continue to guard them until the youngsters reach a size where they can fend for themselves and swim off. Even at this level of life, there is care given to the continuation of the species.

The river itself is part of a great cycle of life. It flows from the mountains in small rivulets, joining other streams, until it becomes this broad river. The variety of life forms supported by the river system is staggering. Life exists at all levels, from the river bottom, to the water column, to its surface and shores. Even as the river flows onward to the bay and ocean, the sun is evaporating water from its surface as well as lakes and the ocean itself. The evaporated water cycles through the atmosphere and will eventually fall as precipitation replenishing the mountain aquifers feeding this and other streams and rivers.

Looking at the river closely, consider the life cycles therein. On the river bottom are the aquatic insects such as mayflies, stoneflies, and caddis flies. These insects are fed upon by the small fishes, minnows and chubs which are in turn are hunted by the predator fish, bass, and walleye. There are also crayfish, turtles, mussels, salamanders, the list is endless. The mayfly nymphs at maturity will swim to the surface; shed their skin and fly away as adults. Their adult life may last only hours; however, they will find a mate and deposit their eggs under the river's surface before dying. With the eggs they deposit, the species will continue. So it is with all species, they are born, grow, live, and pass on their genes to the next generation.

Look at the shoreline, clothed in a variety of aquatic grasses and sedges. These too, rely on the river for moisture and nutrients. As they grow, they are propagating their species through flowering and the production of seeds. Some seeds fall nearby but others are carried by river currents downstream to start new colonies. The plants themselves provide habitat for other species such as dragonflies, damselflies, crayfish, leaches, turtles, frogs and the like, an ecosystem within an ecosystem. Consider the frog who lays her eggs in the shallows. Those eggs hatch as tadpoles with gills, swimming the shallows feeding on aquatic insects. As they mature, they develop legs and lungs, losing their tail. One day, they will crawl onto dry land as frogs like their parents, the passing of genes. All this is, again, a cycle of renewal and life.

Further ashore, the birches, maples and willows have budded and are leafing after a long winter of cold and snow. They were dormant during the cold season but are bursting forth as the days of spring lengthen. Once leafing is complete, the tree's priority is to bloom and seed to further the species. As with the grasses, some seeds fall nearby, and others are carried by the river downstream. For millennia, this has been the survival tactic of these tree species. The shore line has gone from a stark gray to brilliant greens within just several weeks. These shoreline trees are preferred by certain bird species such as the red-winged blackbird. As the trees come into full green, the birds have paired, built nests, and are brooding their offspring. As the eggs hatch, the parents will bring food and raise the young until they are ready to fend for themselves. The cycle of life is prevalent and continues from one generation to the next.

The shoreline itself, which may appear stark, is also the home to unseen life. Muskrats dig channels and tunnels into its bank, building dens for the raising of their young. The shoreline also provides nesting sites for snapping, mud, and other turtles, which crawl out of the water unto the bank to dig their nests, lay eggs, and cover them over. They are then back to the river, relying on the heat of the sun to incubate their offspring. The shoreline is regularly patrolled by minks, raccoons, and porcupines, all looking for food. Indeed, the shoreline of our river is still another ecosystem with an ecosystem.

This concept of life from life, cycles within cycles and ecosystems within ecosystems can be seen far from the river and riverbank. The forests, prairies, mountains, and deserts all adhere to the same process, supporting the life adapted to each ecological niche. At a higher level, the ocean currents, the seasons, even the Earth itself with its tectonic plates are on a cycle of birth and renewal.

Sit on the riverbank and consider what you have seen—that life begets life, that one ecosystem supports another, that everything is within a cycle of renewal and rebirth. Now, turn that insight onto yourself. Is not the care you give your children like the care of the catfish for its young? Is not your heart and blood stream like the river and its tributaries? It has been said that there are more microbes living in and on each human body than there are stars in the Milky Way Galaxy. Your body is like an ecosystem supporting other ecosystems just as we have seen on our river. Does not your body go through cycles on a daily, monthly, and yearly basis just like all else on this planet?

The Earth itself is alive; to all knowledge it is unique in the universe; a planet attuned to the life that it supports. With this insight, I will leave it to the reader to conclude just how such a wonderful world could come into existence, could it be by chance, or is it by design?

So, it seems that the logical answer to the question "What is the meaning of life?" is as follows. "Since we are all an integral part of this beautiful live world, the meaning of life is:

To live a long life;
To be kind and care for others,
To bring them to the realizations that we have discovered;
To learn, enjoy and protect the beauty of this world; and finally,
To raise and educate our young to see the wondrous light
and truths that we see."

Tiger Lilies

During my youth living along the Susquehanna River, every spring we had instances of high water, when the river came over its normal banks and spread across the backyard. As the water receded, it left a line of flotsam at the high-water line. This included a combination of reeds, sticks, bottles, logs, railroad ties, just about anything that had floated down the river. It was my job to clean the mess up, rake, and carry the burnable wood to the garden. The logs and railroad ties, I dragged back to the river and pushed into the current to be carried downstream. One year, I found a set of tubers in the mess. I did not know what kind of plant they were, but was familiar with tulip bulbs and such, so I planted them along one of our stone retaining walls. A few weeks later, sprouts broke through the ground and grew and grew until mid-June, when they developed buds and blossomed into beautiful orange blooms with black dots, tiger lilies. Every year after that, they multiplied and spread until the fronted the entire wall for twenty feet, a wonderful display of color. Like many people today, all the tubers that I found only needed a chance to sink roots, grow, bloom, and multiply, making the world a beautiful place for all.

Horny Chubs

Courtesy of Pixabay

When I was a teen living along the Susquehanna River, I looked forward each spring to the coming of the horny chubs. The true name for these little fish is horned chubs, they are real, look them up. They are named for the small white hornlike projections on their heads. Other than their unusual name, they are not much to see, small, no longer than ten inches. Every May they congregated in the shallows near shore to spawn. They were fascinating to observe. Brightly colored males prepared a spawning nest, excavating a 10-inch diameter depression on the river bottom by moving pebble by pebble with their mouths. The gathered pebbles were stacked around the depression four to six inches high. The male then attracted a female to spawn just over the nest so that her eggs fell and filtered down between the pebbles. The nest was then guarded by the male until the eggs hatched, and the baby fish swam away. When your children are giving you fits, think of this little insignificant fish and the care it gives to its young, can we do any less?

Older Brothers

This is a story of perseverance and fortitude; of growing up in the 1950s with two older brothers who were six and seven years older than myself. My name is Larry, and I grew up in a small Pennsylvania river town living on the wrong side of the railroad tracks. I had two brothers, Ron (six years) and Paul (seven years) older than myself.

For the first six years of my life, I was basically ignored by my older brothers. They were only one year apart in age, and were content to play together and ignore me, or push me aside. This was apparently fine with me because I carry no scars, psychologically or physically from this period. They were probably the best years of my early life.

My first firm recollection of them occurred when I was about six. We lived on the shore of the Susquehanna River, and my brothers were into fishing. It was spring, and the river was high and roily from the annual spring rains, and the fishing for carp and catfish was good. Near my home, built into the shores of the river, was an old concrete pier used by coal dredges and barges during the early part of the twentieth century. It was a popular fishing spot during high water, because it jutted into the flow and created slack water for the fish to hold and feed. Every night, a small crowd of locals gathered, started a roaring fire, and fished from the edge of the pier. My brothers, then twelve and thirteen, were getting their gear together, and I wanted to go along. My parents refused my request, because the gang sat on the edge of the pier overlooking the swirling waters, potentially dangerous if one slipped off the wall. I begged, and finally, my brothers vowed that they would not let me get onto the pier, but rather stay behind it, where it was safe. My parents relented and away we went. When we got to the pier, my brothers set their fishing poles and lifted me on the pier to sit on the edge with them; my parents never knew our secret. I thought then that this was very kind of them, but now, I am not sure they were not trying to get rid of me. I could visualize it,

"Sorry Mom, Larry wouldn't listen to us and slipped off the pier. It is okay though, he said he wondered what it would be like to swim with the fishes."

This was the beginning of the torture. The older that I became, the more wary of their motives I grew. In the summer when fishing near our house, they waded, and urged me into deeper and deeper water. This led to my self-taught swimming style comprised mostly of arm flailing, leg kicking and gasping for air.

My father was a trackman on the Pennsylvania Railroad and attended an annual union-sponsored picnic with the family. One of the activities was a scramble for nickels hidden in a pile of sawdust. In those days, a nickel was worth something and attracted a lot of attention. Most of the kids were much older than me and experienced at pushing aside youngsters. As the result I was quickly pushed and pummeled in the mad dash for the coins and found myself trampled face down with a mouth full of sawdust. At least, when I bit down, I found the only nickel I got for my pain. During the rush, my brothers were nowhere to be found for protection. This event left me with a psychological aversion of crowds that I have only recently overcome.

Sometimes in the winter when there was snow on the ground, they invited me to go sledding with them. They usually let me take the first run, down the large hill near the house that sloped to the river shore. On a good run, the trail went down the hill, across a backyard, and onto the frozen river ice. When I got older, I realized that they were using me to test the trail, to make sure there were no protruding rocks or trees that could not be steered around. They also made me the guinea pig to see if the ice was thick enough to support their weight. These activities left me with a psychological aversion to being first at anything. To this day, I refuse to be the first one on a plane, or to sit in the front seat of an amusement park ride, or even sit in the front pew at church.

Being the youngest and smallest brother, all the chores fell on me. I was the one who had to fill the coal buckets daily, shovel the snow, dig the garden, whatever needed done. Paul and Ron just had a knack of disappearing or "being busy" when something needed done. My only way of getting back was to tattle when they were up to something; I knew where they hid their cigarettes; I knew when they were sneaking out at night and where they were going; I even knew when they were skipping school. What I knew, our parents knew, this was my only way to level the playing field.

In the 1950s, with limited television and no computer games or cell phones, my brothers regularly joined other boys in the neighborhood for games of football or baseball. I, of course, was much too small and young to participate. I was relegated to the back steps to watch and cheer. If I was lucky, I was allowed to retrieve foul balls from the vacant lot adjacent to the ball field. I was allowed this involvement because that lot was grown up with weeds, poison sumac, poison oak, poison ivy, itch weed, briers, thorn bushes, and snakes. I regularly came home with scratches, nicks, and rashes from the poisons, but luckily no snake bites. I spent so much time in that poison-infested lot that to this day I am immune to poison ivy and such, they hold no power over me. Of course, this means that whenever my wife is weeding and sees a plant that has leaves in a group of three, she calls me from whatever I am doing to get rid of it.

Not every aspect of living with my brothers was bad. My parents were glad that after two evil sons, they had a son who was not out to destroy or rule the world. This meant that I got to ride in the front seat on car trips instead of in the back with the raucous pair. Mom always gave me the first piece of her cherry custard pies. This attention was not overlooked by Paul and Ron, who plotted to get even with me. Day fishing trips in the old leaky wooden rowboat were the worst. First, I was forced to hunt bait for the day by digging for worms in the garden. Then, I was set to rowing the boat to likely holes, where I was made to fish on the "wrong" side of the boat so that I was unlikely to catch anything. The saving grace here is that I was and still am a much better fisherman than either brother, and always managed to best them at the end of the day. On one memorable day, my brother Ron and I were going to fish the "hole" behind the house. After I finished digging bait, we began wading to the small gravelly island at the edge of the "hole." Ron was ahead of me and kept calling me to follow into the deeper water, to cross to get to the island. I followed cautiously, of course leery of, first, why he had invited me to fish with him in the first place; second, why he sounded so friendly and nice; and third, why he was so far in front of me and calling me to hurry. I had my old broken fishing rod and reel, and no live bait, because Ron said that I would do better with the huge red and white spoon lure that he had tied on the end of my line. As I advanced step by careful step, I began casting my lure towards the small pocket just below the island. Suddenly, there was a jolt, and my old rod bent double. Luckily, I was still wading relatively shallow water, or the fish could have pulled me to my doom; which may have been Ron's plan. My fishing line was like rope and held well; and after much time I was able to drag the fish to shore. It was a Northern Pike, one of only two or three I have ever caught in the Susquehanna. Ron never caught any. It was the largest fish of my young life and not to be exceeded for at least two years. I managed to drag it to the house and present it to my mother, who cleaned it and prepared it for supper. After eating, mom gave me a piece of cherry custard pie when nobody was looking, and I retired to the back porch to sit on the porch swing and revel in my achievements for the day. Even as I ate, I knew that someplace nearby, my brothers were smoking cigarettes and plotting to get back at me for my success.

During these early days we had a chicken coop on the property. This was before there were ordinances against livestock in town, and many people raised chickens. We did not have a lot of chickens, maybe twenty-five or so. Of course, one of my daily chores was feeding the birds and gathering eggs. This consisted of filling a bucket with chicken feed, entering the fenced in chicken yard, and scattering the feed for the birds. When the bucket was empty, while the chickens were eating, I gathered eggs in the bucket. Most of the chickens were hens but there were one or two roosters all the time. One felt protective of the hens and did not like me. It seems that my brothers taunted him regularly and he became meaner and meaner. One day, when I entered the chicken yard, he attacked me and thoroughly flogged me. I went crying to the house, more scared than injured, and told my story. My father gathered his ax and headed to the chicken yard; we had roast chicken with all the trimmings for dinner that night. After dinner, Mom gave me a huge piece of apple pie when nobody was looking and I headed for the porch swing, satisfied with the day.

As I was approaching my early teens, Paul and Ron discovered that there was more to life than ruling and destroying the world. There were girls. My karma increased during this period as theirs waned. They spent hours in front of the mirror brushing their hair this way or that as though the position of a single strand of hair would make them attractive or an abomination. This was the height of rock and roll, so the AM radio was blaring nearby. Being twelve years old or so, I was full of myself and stood behind them, mocking their every move. For some reason, they would suddenly turn to smack me or chase me. Of course, I was much too nimble to catch, my reactions honed from years of just surviving. I ducked or sidestepped or back pedaled, or whatever it took to avoid the blow. As soon as they turned back to the mirror, I was back in place, combing my crew cut with my fingers.

Soon, they were married and living on their own, beginning their own families. I missed them for about the first 15 seconds or so; then began reallocating available living space to meet my needs. I had much planning to do if I was going to rule and destroy the world.

Susquehanna River Sledding

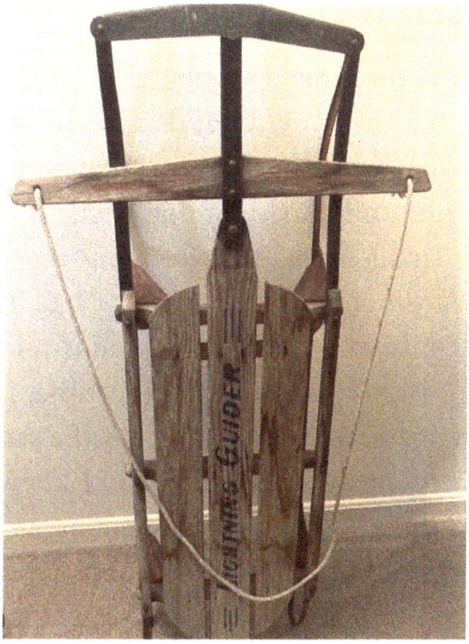

Author's childhood Lightning Glider sled from the 1950s.

My preteens in the 1950s was a time of numerous heavy winter snows; the schools were closed for days at a time. My best friend and I spent these days sledding the many small hills in the neighborhood. There was one particularly long, steep hill where we decided to lay out a sledding course. We spent the whole day stamping down the snow, moving rocks and tree branches brought down by an earlier ice storm. At last we were ready, we mounted our sleds in tandem and down we went. As we neared the bottom of our prepared trail, we realized that we were moving much too fast to stop, and just beyond the end of the trail was the Susquehanna River, icy but not yet frozen over. We had to steer our sleds into a riverside brush pile full of thorns to avoid a disastrous icy plunge. The moral is, when you are laying out an important plan in your life, make sure that you are not heading for disaster.

Great Danes that I have Known

You may think that this discourse deals with people from Denmark (Danes), but that would not be true. In this case, I am talking about a dog that I met while growing up that was of the Great Dane breed. I will get back to this particular dog later.

I grew up in a small railroad town along the Susquehanna River during the 1950s. As an enterprising youth, I had a paper route which gave me the opportunity to interact with various canines, some friendly, some not so friendly. At my home during this time, I can remember two dogs, although I do not think we had them at the same time.

The first was a little beagle named Lassie. I knew Lassie was named after the collie from the TV show by the same name, but our Lassie was not a collie and was not even female. This gave great consternation to one neighbor lady who insisted on calling him Laddie instead of Lassie.

Lassie was an outside dog with a dog house and chain. My father grew up on the farm and did not believe in inside dogs. I am not sure why we had a dog; we never took Lassie hunting for rabbits, and he was not a protector, but I enjoyed playing with him. The only problem was, if you left Lassie off his leash, he would take off and not be seen for at least three days. Lassie lived a long life and was a great companion.

Sometime afterwards, my father brought home a stray that we named Rex. Rex was basically a mongrel, large and muscular, with long hair. Where Lassie was timid, Rex thought of himself as the owner of the world. He was friendly to the family but aggressive to outsiders. Rex's best quality was his strength. In the winter, I could tie him to my sled, and he would pull me around the backyard.

Most of my dog acquaintances were on my paper route. Riding home on my bike from the end of my paper route one day, a large mongrel ran out from a house, grabbed my leg, and held on. I had never seen him before this day, and I was in a lot of pain. Somehow, I was able to ride fast enough to lose him and make it home. The doctor was concerned about rabies but decided against a series of painful shots unless symptoms appeared. Luckily, they did not, but it took several weeks for the wounds to heal.

Near the end of our dead-end street, I had a paper customer with a collie named Skip. Skip hated me and would come charging to the door snarling whenever I collected for the paper. This went on for several years, no matter how much I tried talking to Skip to win him over. One day when I stopped, they had a second dog, a black Labrador puppy named Nancy. Nancy and I hit it off right away. Now when I collected, Skip snarled and barked like always, but Nancy was allowed out the door to accompany me to the end of the street and back, playing fetch or just walking by my side. We went on like this for a while, but then there came a change in Skip's reaction to me. Gradually, he came to the door with Nancy, with his tail wagging, and no snarling and no barking. Eventually, he was allowed out as well and both dogs would play with me to the end of the street. Both dogs remained my good friends until the day I gave up the paper route.

Another family on my route had a large mixed breed named Max that never accepted me. He snapped and snarled every time I came to the door. This family liked their paper delivered to the back door which was down a concrete enclosed stairway to a lower-level patio. One day, I started down the stairs and was shocked to see Max run around the corner and at me. He had me all to himself in the stairwell. All I could do is stick out my foot and put my shoe broadside in his mouth every time he attacked. He could not get around my foot and I could not leave the stairwell; it was a standoff. I yelled as loud as I could for help, and eventually the owner came around the corner to my rescue. He grabbed the dog and dragged him back into the house, while I sat down on the steps shaking uncontrollably. I swear that my short life flashed in front of me every time the dog attacked but the only damage that I had to show was tooth marks in my shoe's sole.

This brings me back to the Great Dane. Eric was a Great Dane kept by the family who lived in the very last house on the street. Eric also did not like me (or anybody) and came crashing through the house barking whenever I collected. Luckily, I never saw Eric outside the house (I do not know where he did his business), until early one Sunday morning when I was marching up the street to deliver the morning paper. Eric was out that morning and saw me. He came bounding down the street like a horse, barking at me. I was terrified and just froze; I thought my life was over. The owner saw what was happening and yelled to me to not run. I thought, *Run.* I was petrified stiff. *How could I run, let alone outrun this horse of a dog, nope, my life was done.* Eric came to me, then stopped, and started sniffing. I just trembled. The owner again yelled for me not to run as he came down the street. I thought that I was lucky just to still be on my feet and in one piece. Eventually, the owner was able to put a leash on Eric and lead him away along with his paper. I just walked home in a daze thinking that there must be a better way for a teenager to make money, maybe like defusing bombs.

Susquehanna Riverbed Rocks

If you drive along the Susquehanna, especially when the water levels are lower, you cannot help seeing the rock ledges and falls that spread from shore to shore. These are the bed rocks at the base of mountains that have been eroded away over the lifetime of the river, some sixty million years. These rock ledges are solid; they have seen unimaginable floods; they will be as they are for millions of years into the future. You should be lucky enough to have just one or two friends as solid as these rocks for they will be your anchors, dependable for the ages.

First Discovery

Author, age 10 (1957) with Susquehanna carp

My earliest experience with the Susquehanna River was during the early 1950s when I was six or seven years old. My family lived in an old house on the wrong side of the railroad tracks. The railroad tracks were very close to the house, less than one hundred feet from the front door, very loud and dirty. The railroad right-of-way was sided with our street, North Main. While the street climbed and descended hills, the railroad was leveled with a retaining wall where the street was lower, as was the case in the front of our house. Next to the wall ran Main Street, our narrow front yard and then the house. The house was built on the side of a hill slopping to the river so that, in effect, the house had four floors. The top two floors were at street level and above, the next down, basically the kitchen was on the side of the hill, and finally the lower level which was the foundation and cellar. It was exposed on the river side and sat on a level about eight feet above the river's normal flood plain. The kitchen level had a large, raised porch attached, that gave an excellent view of the river, and was a joy during the summer.

I had two older brothers, and with the river so close, they spent much of their time fishing, boating, and swimming. The Susquehanna River in those days was not very clean; many towns saw no problem in dumping their raw sewage into its waters. Nevertheless, it was alive with all manner of life, from mayflies to many species of fish, including black bass, carp, catfish, sunfish, rock bass, pike, walleye, and various chubs. During spates of high water, much debris could be seen floating by from the back porch. Sometimes, lost or abandoned wooden rowboats were seen, and my brothers and I sprang into action to attempt a salvage. Usually, these were worn out craft, badly damaged, rotted or just leaky, but when I found one, I would attempt repairs to make it serviceable.

High water usually occurred during the early spring, with snow melt and heavy rains. These flood waters usually concentrated much of the river's fish population near shore, where currents were slower and easy food could be found on the flooded terrain. My brothers spent most evenings camped out along the shore line, with fishing poles set on forked sticks, waiting for a passing catfish or carp. They also had a roaring campfire nearby, to provide light and to ward off the damp evening chill. Sometimes groups of six to ten fishermen gathered at a particularly good spot to share the fire, fishing, storytelling, and good times.

One of the popular fishing spots was known as the steamboat landing. It was an old concrete abutment built on the shore of the Susquehanna River at the turn of the twentieth century. Its original function was as a mooring and offloading facility for dredges, which plied the river pulling coal from the river bottom. By the 1950s, it had not seen service for many years. As its bulk jutted out into the river's current, it created a large eddy that attracted many fish and fishermen on the downstream side.

My brothers visited the landing most evenings during high water, but because I was so small and young I was not allowed to accompany them. They sat on the wall of the landing with their feet dangling fifteen feet above the fast water. My parents thought that I was just too small to join them. The landing also had a concrete setback cut into its side that allowed water to circulate to and from the main river, but was without current or high walls. For my first trip to the landing, my brothers convinced my parents that they would watch me closely and I would only fish in the setback. Needless to say; I did not fish there; I was sitting on the wall with everybody else. There was a large fire blazing, and I had a great time. I recall catching a large rock bass on the order of twelve inches long. From that time, I was allowed to accompany my brothers on a regular basis, but we never told my parents that I was fishing from the wall.

Hurricanes

Hurricanes were a common occurrence during the 1950s. It seemed that we were hit with the big storms every year. The first one that I can remember was Hurricane Hazel in 1954, when I was about eight years old. My strongest memory is of sitting in the dark living room at night huddled with the family, while the wind and rain pounded our old house along the river. For some reason, it seemed that these storms always struck at night. Maybe they did not really, but one's most vivid memories are formed in the dark of night when the mind visualizes what the eyes cannot see.

Darkness was what we had, the electricity was long out, and the room was lit by only the flames of several kerosene lamps. Outside, we heard the howling of the wind, the beating of the rain, all punctuated by bangs and crashes that could not be identified. The wind and rain built in intensity all evening until around midnight. Suddenly, all was calm; the rain stopped, and the wind died. The change from storm to calm was almost instantaneous. We ventured out the front door to investigate. We found that we were in the eye of the storm; the air was humid and warm with the stars shining above. It was eerie and hard to believe that the maelstrom still continued on all sides of our little island of calm.

After a short period of time, the wind started picking up again from the opposite direction as the storm's eye passed on. We then had to endure the second half of the storm, although it was not as severe as the first. In the morning, we surveyed the damage. One corner of our galvanized tin roof had blown loose and was pushed up. A little more storm and we may have lost most of, or our entire, roof. As it was, it was repaired without too much effort. Our backyard was littered with tree limbs of various sizes from our maple trees, but the trees themselves had survived the storm in good condition. Several of the neighbors had mature maple trees uprooted and laying on their sides. One of the lingering effects of these storms were the floods and high water on the Susquehanna River which rose over the next several days.

What the hurricane represented was part of a huge natural cycle. This storm had developed in the tropics near the west coast of Africa. It had crossed thousands of miles of open ocean before reaching Pennsylvania. During its voyage, as it grew and intensified, the storm absorbed billions of gallons of sea water into its circulation. As the storm died over land, all this water fell to the Earth as rain, which flowed into creeks, which flowed into small rivers, which flowed into the Susquehanna River, and hence back to the Chesapeake Bay; and ultimately the Atlantic Ocean from which it had originated.

Home and TV

Author at age three with favorite toy (that he still has to this day)

Growing up during the 1950s, all that seemed important was to get my school homework finished so that I could sit in front of the new wonder in the house, the 21-inch black and white television set. Before TV, our entertainment was to sit around the large floor model radio in the evening and listen to the news, comedy, drama, and entertainment broadcasts. I can remember shows such as *Gunsmoke*, *The Shadow*, *Art Linkletter*, and others. The radio was okay, but with the TV, we had three channels to choose from. Imagine that, three sometimes snowy, sometimes wavy channels to watch. There were the three primary networks, NBC, CBS, and ABC, each with one station in our area from which to choose. NBC came in with the best reception; it was a VHF station, and most times was crisp and sharp. VHF stood for Very High Frequency and there were 13 VHS channels on the selector plus 72 UHF channels. UHF stood for Ultra High Frequency, which I guess was even higher than Very High Frequency. The CBS channel was second best, wavy only occasionally, but the ABC channel was always snowy, sometimes almost impossible to watch. If one of the three networks did not carry a show or event, it was not worth watching. Best of all, they broadcast all day. No, not 24 hours around the clock, but all day, as in 5:00 a.m. until signoff at midnight. At signoff time, they broadcasted a picture of the US flag waving in the breeze while the national anthem played. As the anthem ended, the picture switched to that beautiful snow.

At some time during this period, there was an advertisement aired for a plastic film that would transform a black and white TV into a color set. The advertisement talked about how wonderful it would be to watch your TV and see blue sky and green grass. This sounded like a good investment, so I sent my $5.95 to the post office box advertised and, in a few weeks, received the advertised plastic film. It did indeed allow the family to see blue sky and green grass. You see, the film was tinted blue on the top and green on the bottom and sort of a light brown in between. When placed on the front of the TV screen (it adhered via static electricity), and if the show being aired had blue sky and green grass, that is what you saw. If, however, the show being aired was, say indoors with people talking, the people had blue hair and green clothes. This was one of the first TV rip-offs, a tradition that continues to this day.

The broadcast day started out with local news, and farm reports (farm reports were important in those days), then the network news shows. The most popular early news show was *The Today Show*, which regularly featured a stupid chimpanzee. After the news shows came the morning game shows, *Let's Make a Deal* was always my favorite. Contestants could win fabulous prizes, worth hundreds of dollars, a small fortune to me. The afternoons were all about the soaps. Many of the soap operas began as radio shows and were brought to the new media as TV became more common. My mother always made sure that she had her cleaning done so she would not miss a minute of *The Edge of Night*, not ever. I can still see her sitting in her rocker, hankie in hand for those everyday sad events when some character learned that they were dying, yet again. After the soaps, when we kids were coming home from school, were the afternoon cartoon shows with Porky, Bugs, Road Runner, and the rest of the animated gang. This was the time for *The Mickey Mouse Club*, which I did not miss for years. I grew up with Annette, Corky, and the rest, but we could not afford to buy the Mickey ears.

As evening came, it was back to the news from 6 to 7 p.m., local, then the national with reports from around the globe, often with just the voice of the reporter, no "live" camera shots. The national news could be scary with stories about the Soviet nuclear threat, or wars raging in Africa or Asia. This was the time that I first heard of "gorilla" warfare. I knew about the chimp on the Today show, and just could not understand how a gorilla could be smart enough to pick up and use a gun, and what for, bananas? With all the worry about the Soviets and the arms race, we had regular air raid drills in school, crawling under our desks for protection from nuclear attack. Now, how much protection would a wooden desk give in a nuclear blast? Anyway, we kids did not like to think about the possibilities. Finally, after the news, was prime time TV! *Ed Sullivan, the Lucy Show, Jack Benny, the Honeymooners*, classics today. To me, TV was neat, but not overwhelming, I grew up with it. I now wonder what my parents thought about it. They grew up on the farm with hand pumped water, outhouses, and kerosene lamps. To them, the leap from the nineteenth century to the middle of the twentieth century must have been marvelous.

Susquehanna River, for the Ages

The Susquehanna River runs generally north to south from southern New York through Pennsylvania and Maryland to the Chesapeake Bay. The river is said to have been flowing for the last 60 million years. Most rivers follow mountain valleys, but this river is a notable exception, it regularly cuts through mountain ridges north to south. This is because the river predates the mountain ridges. As the ridges rose, the river kept its course and cut through the rising land. The rocks that you see in the image above, are in fact the bare bones of mountains that have been traversed and subdued. The river was also once much longer than now; what is now the Chesapeake Bay was the lower river valley that was flooded as the oceans rose after the last ice age. Like the river, once you set goals for your life, persevere in your efforts for success.

Nature of Sleep

Sleep is like the vast, dark, and mysterious forest interrupted only by the rivers of dreams. It extends on to the bright shining sea, the coming of the awakening.

Submarines and Rafts

Growing up on the shores of the Susquehanna River presented me with a variety of adventures without getting into too much trouble. Summertime was the best, school was out, days were long and warm, and the river ran low and clear. My best friend, Steve, and I lived the lives of Huckleberry Finn and Tom Sawyer. Up early in the morning with a quick breakfast, we were out of our homes until dark.

At some time during the day, a sure bet was that the nearby river would attract our attention. The possibilities were endless. Maybe we would decide to throw sticks in the current and then try to hit them with rocks. Throwing rocks accurately when you are twelve is important, and the rocks were everywhere along the river bank. On hot days, to cool off, we started out wading in the shallows near shore. This was our private part of the river, bordered upstream and downstream by two large boulders; that we named imaginatively as First Rock and Second Rock. The water was no more than two to three feet deep there.

When we were younger (ten), it was all the further in the river we were allowed to go, so it was our swimming hole. Beyond the two boulders were two small islands that only became islands when the river was at its lowest stages. They were named First Island and Second Island. If nothing else, we were consistent in our naming conventions. They were gravel bars that had been created by ice jams sometime in the geologic past. The ice gouged out the river bottom and deposited the material in piles that became the islands. Second Island was furthest from shore, and beyond it, was "The Hole."

The Hole was the trench that the ice had gouged to create the island. It was maybe one hundred feet long by fifty feet wide and relatively deep, over six feet in some spots. It was the deepest water for some distance around and attracted the largest fish to its cool dark depths. Between the Second Rock and Second Island, another pool had been gouged, much smaller and shallower than The Hole. Material gouged from this pool had become First Island. This pool was about twenty-five feet in diameter and three feet or so in depth. In the center was a huge boulder of a rough aggregate material much different from the sandstone most of the river's rocks were composed of. I often wondered about its makeup. It must have been millions, or maybe billions of years old; how did it come to be placed where it was in the middle of my little world? This pool became our second swimming hole after we had outgrown the one between the two rocks. This pool became the site of our great submarine and raft adventures.

There was always a large pile of used lumber underneath the raised back porch. This pile contained boards of various widths, lengths, and thicknesses, the remains of construction and repair projects around the homestead over the years, from new porches to chicken pen repairs. This pile provided materials for the building projects that Steve and I took on. We decided that we needed a water craft of our own. Boats were much too complicated so we decided that we would build ourselves a raft. Two-by-sixes became the frame of our craft. On top were nailed various shapes and dimensions of leftover lumber, whatever we could find.

It was a major time-consuming project for us boys; we must have spent two or three hours putting it together. What we did not think about was how we were going to get the finished raft to the river. We had it all assembled; it was very primitive, but it looked really a neat thing to a twelve-year-old. A rope was tied to one end (I bought rope by the mile), which was later to serve as a tether for the anchor. We gave a mighty pull in the direction of the river, but nothing moved. It was all we could do to budge it a few inches; it was so very heavy.

Being young and creative, we put our Radio Flyer wagons to use. With great effort we lifted the ends, one at a time, onto our wagons. The wagon wheels wanted to sink into the soft soil under the grass, but we were able to transport our creation to the river bank. The wagons allowed us to pull it right into the river until it floated free. It did float, although with all the weight, it floated very low in the water. Then for the great event, as one we climbed on board our worthy craft. It went straight to the bottom; it did not have the buoyancy to support our scant weight. A raft that did not float is not of much use, so it was back to the drawing board.

We knew that things filled with air floated very well. In addition to floating sticks, we often targeted floating soda bottles with our rocks. With that knowledge, we pulled our raft back out of the water, which required even greater effort than launching it, now that it was uphill from the water. We flipped it over to dry and headed to one of the town's gasoline service stations with our wagons. An hour later, we were back and commenced pounding again. Soon, we were launching our craft again and were elated to find that it floated like a top, even with both of us on board.

What did we do, you ask? Why did we visit the service station? The answer was simple; we collected all the two-gallon oil cans that our wagons could carry. They were made of tin or some metal and had sealable caps. We arranged them in rows inside the two-by-six wooden frame from underneath the raft, and nailed boards to keep them in place without puncturing them. They gave the raft the lift that it needed and we were thrilled. The raft became the center of our river activities for the summer.

That same summer, my parents had to replace our water heater. This must have been about the same time that home insulation was discovered. The new water heater was enclosed in an insulating wrap of fiberglass for efficiency. The old heater, on the other hand, was a big bare metal tube with pipes sticking out of the top of it. I guess that it had a heating element someplace, but I do not remember any electrical connections. Anyway, I asked my dad if I could have it; I was making plans already. Steve and I drained the remaining water from it and plugged the pipe ends with wooden stoppers that we whittled out of the wood pile. It was easy to get to the river, just turn it sideways and roll, roll, roll. It was so heavy that it did not float very well, just barely above the surface. When one of us laid on it, it floated just under the surface like a submarine. It even had a periscope of sorts in the form of one of the pipes that came out of the side and curved to the top. We spent hours pretending that the raft was an aircraft carrier being attacked by the water heater submarine, and we had great fun.

All good things come to an end, however. As the summer was ending, a passing hurricane or tropical storm unleashed heavy rains. We had not moved our craft to higher ground beforehand and the rising river waters washed both our craft away. The loss did not bother us for long however, summer was over, and the river was turning cold, it was time for us to turn our attention to our next adventure.

Close Encounters of a Susquehanna River Kind

When I was younger, a good friend and I were fishing the Susquehanna River for bass. We were wading along a ledge near shore, casting to deeper water on either side. Suddenly my friend, who was ahead of me, did a little dance and hurried in my direction. I asked him if he tripped or slipped, but he said that he was wading, looked down, and there was a snake swimming by near the bottom. I told him not to worry; it was just a harmless water snake looking for any food that we might stir up. We kept going and he moved forward again. We fished for a while, and he turned to me and said, "Wow, another snake just swam on the top of the water, between my legs. Those water snakes are sure busy today."

I replied that I had seen the snake also, it was a poisonous copperhead and that it was good that he did not harass it. His smile changed to a gasp and his eyes bulged. He asked, "How do you know it was a copperhead, and the first snake just a harmless water snake?" I told him that the old man next door told me how to tell; water snakes are designed to swim underwater and so they do. On the other hand, copperheads are land snakes and always swim high on the surface; they do not really like the water. I explained that I regularly mowed the old man's lawn, and he would make us sandwiches. While we ate, we discussed the river, the fish, the birds, and everything else imaginable. The moral is that there is much to learn from older people, they have accumulated a lifetime of knowledge, so listen to them.

The Lazy Days of Summer

During the long lazy summer days of the late 1950s, life was good for a twelve-year-old growing up in the small Pennsylvania railroad town. My family lived along the Susquehanna River in an old frame house that was cold in the winter and hot in the summer. These were the days before air conditioning when relief from the heat came from a cool drink in the shade of the huge maple tree in the side yard or a long swim in the cool waters of the river. The Susquehanna River was always inviting; and most days were spent on or in the water, boating, fishing, swimming, or all three at once. The fishing was outstanding in those days; this was before the sport became competitive. As a preteen, it did not matter to me what I caught, a carp was as much fun as a bass, and maybe more so.

On many warm summer nights, I slept on the back porch to escape the heat that had not yet dissipated from the house. The back porch was elevated ten feet above ground level and provided a view of the big backyard that sloped to the river shore. The evening was full of sounds, frogs and toads along the river bank, as well as a million insects not seen. As the night progressed, the sounds tapered off until there was dead silence just before the first light of dawn; then the birds started their morning serenade. As the night progressed, it also got colder and damper in my make-do bed, an old mattress. I was glad for every blanket that I could wrap around myself to keep out the chill.

At first light, I gathered my fishing gear and head to the river. My old wooden boat was salvaged from the river during the previous spring's high water. It was very old and worn out. When I found it, one side had a large crack, but I had managed to patch it with a piece of tin and roofing nails covered with lots of tar. Even patched, it still leaked between the floor boards, so the first chore was to bail the river water that had invaded overnight. I never wore good shoes to the river; that was the place for old sneakers with holes where toes could breathe fresh air. The river during the early morning was magical. The water was smooth and subdued, not yet disturbed by the wind. The air was heavy, cool, and damp with fog often hugging the surface of the water. Sounds did not carry well in the heavy air, rowing the boat through the flat misty water was like being in a dream. Ducks and geese were not yet alert; it was easy to row within a few feet before they scattered to find solitude elsewhere.

The fishing during those early morning jaunts was never as good as I expected. It seemed that the fish were sluggish and did not want to see the new day. Sometimes, however, it was possible to sneak up on very large fish in very shallow water. The bass moved into the shallows overnight to stalk small fish and crayfish, and were slow to return to deeper water. They would suddenly realize that there was a large dark presence just overhead and take off like a bullet, leaving a wake as they shot off into the cover of the nearest deep water.

There were other fishers astir in those early hours. There was another fisherman from the local area enjoying the solitude, as well as an aerial assault by ospreys hunting for breakfast to feed themselves and their nestlings. It is amazing to watch an osprey working a section of river. They fly into the wind at an altitude of several hundred feet, watching for the shadow of an unsuspecting fish, usually a sucker. The translucent scales of a fish make them difficult to see, but their shadow is a dead giveaway as to their presence. When an osprey spots something that looks like a fish, they hover in midair to confirm their target. They then fold their wings and dive from above. At the last moment, just before entering the water, they pull their talons forward and plunge into the water with a large splash. As they take back to the air with the captured quarry, they turn the fish in their claws, head first so it is aerodynamic for flight. With breakfast in claw, the osprey soars off to its nest on the Blue Mountain ridge.

After a couple of hours on the water, the sun rose over the mountain and warmed the world. The mist burned off the water and the breeze rose, and it was time to head for home. I pulled the boat to the shore, unloaded my gear and headed for the house. The time in the open air and the warm sun left me feeling tired again. The rest of the family was still sleeping, so I crawled back into my bed on the porch and was soon in dreamland.

The Rockville Bridge

The Rockville Bridge, which crosses the Susquehanna River north of Harrisburg, is the longest stone arch bridge in the world. Construction was completed in 1902; its forty-eight spans, each seventy feet long, carries four tracks of the Pennsylvania Railroad across the river. It is the railroad's main route to the western part of the state. Other stone pier bridges have been built over the river, only to fail as did the Walnut Street Bridge in Harrisburg, which partially collapsed during flooding in 1996. The reason that the Rockville Bridge has stood so firm was discovered when there was a train accident on the bridge that damaged a pier. It was then learned that the piers were solid stone masonry on the inside as well as the outside. Other bridges such as the Walnut Street Bridge in Harrisburg have solid stone masonry on the outside but were just filled with rubble on the inside. The moral is that it is good to present a solid façade, but it is more important what you are made of on the inside, for this gives you the strength for greatness.

Winter Time

Pennsylvania winters during the 1950s produced some terrible weather; yet were the best of all times to me. When you were a preteen growing up in a small Pennsylvania town, a snow storm, especially a bad snow storm, was just wonderful. I would run from window to window, watching the drifts build in the front yard or on the back porch roof. If the storm was at night, I used my trusty 5 cell flashlight to peer out the bedroom window, making sure that the snow was still falling. There were also trips up the cold attic steps to look out the small window towards the street lamp that stood just down the street. The next morning was a time for early rising, and checking the local radio station for news for school closings. During those years severe winter storms were common, dropping as much as two feet of snow. School was closed for several days to a week while the rural county roads were cleared. It was nice to sit around the small coal stove that stood in our living room enjoying the heat it threw while the storm raged.

The morning after a snow was a time of glee, of putting on two pairs of pants, my heaviest jacket, and a hat with ear muffs. Once the walkway and street parking area were cleared, it was time for fun. Sleds were brought out of their summer storage in the back cellar; and the runners were sanded to remove the rust from nonuse. My best friend lived just next door, and we had several hills that we liked to sled. After a big snow, the easiest was on the street where we lived. Just down the street was a modest hill that had been plowed of the deep snow and packed by local traffic. The streetlight was at the bottom of the hill and provided light for night sledding. If we were lucky, no cinders had been scattered on the pavement, and the snow was packed hard and icy. The hill was not high or steep but provided an acceptable ride. Of course, the occasional traffic was something to watch out for. On more than one occasion, as the snow began to melt or cinders were spread, we shoveled snow from the shoulders and repack the base. Drivers in the cars that went past, for some reason, did not seem to appreciate our efforts to keep the hill icy. If the hill was especially slippery, we could make it to the gate at our side yard, which led down a small slope to the side of the house. Making the turn added another fifty feet to the run. We had to be careful though, the hill either ended at the house, or at an eight-foot drop over a stone retaining wall to another property level.

At the far side of my friend's property was another hill that we used, that began at the side of their garage and ran into the backyard toward the Susquehanna River. It also was not very steep, but my friend's dad, on cold days, sprinkled it with water to make ice. The ice made it incredibly fast; and we constructed a ramp of snow and ice so we could make small but bone-jarring jumps.

Several houses down the street at the top of the hill on the street where we sledded lived an elderly couple who were like adopted grandparents to us. We often visited and were treated to cookies and hot cocoa. The property sloped steeply, on the back side, to the river. We set up our fastest sled run there. From halfway up the hill, the run started at a 45-degree angle to a gentler slope that ended with a water hazard, the Susquehanna River.

If the river was frozen over, as it often was during winter in the 1950s, it was possible to sled right onto the river ice. Luckily, we avoided doing this, my friend and I never ventured onto the ice, as its thickness and safety was unpredictable. Some places it might be two feet thick, yet twenty feet away it could only be two inches, depending on currents and the structure of the bottom underneath. I think we learned this by trying to throw rocks to slide across the ice. Sometimes the rock seemed to slide forever; sometimes it broke through the ice on contact. It was a dangerous thing sledding down a steep hill towards a cold river, whether it was frozen or not. I doubt that many parents would allow their children to have a sled run that ended at the edge of an icy river today.

Icicles are another memory from the old home. The house had no rain gutters, as only the "rich" had gutters in those days. The snow fell on the various roofs and gradually melted from the heat escaping from the poorly insulated house or warmth from the sun, even though the air temperature was below freezing. As the melted water dripped from the edge of the roof, icicles formed and grew longer and larger. It was not unusual to have icicles that were three to four feet long.

I enjoyed being on the raised back porch, pulling icicles from the edge of the roof and throwing them across the backyard, especially if there had been an ice storm with freezing rain. The icicles shattered upon hitting the frozen crust, into a hundred pieces that slid in all directions. Icicles were also good to suck on, clean and pure, just like a popsicle, only with no flavor. As the weather warmed enough for the icicles to lose their grip on the edge of the roof, they fell with a tremendous crash. More than once, I was struck by falling icicles while playing; luckily with no severe damage done.

As I mentioned earlier, there was a small coal stove in our living room. It was known as a "bucket a day" stove, because that is about how much coal it would burn on a typical winter day. It put out enough heat to keep the living room toasty, but the hallway and bedroom on the same floor were noticeably cooler. In fact, that bedroom was my folks', and they often kept an electric space heater running to keep the temperature tolerable. The living room was situated on the second floor, as the house was built on the side of the hill leading from street level to river level.

The first floor was made up mostly by the kitchen. We had a large cast-iron cook stove which provided heat as well as cooking uses. It could burn either wood or coal, but coal required less attention. I loved the kitchen stove. There was usually a kettle of water on one of the burners for coffee, hot chocolate or washing dishes. When coming in from a long hard cold day playing in the snow, wet boots, socks, pants, hats, and whatever else were left by the stove to dry, which they did quickly. The clothes, when dry, were there, toasty, and warm, waiting for the next outdoor adventure.

The cast-iron burners were great for the creation of flash-fried treats. Bread slices tossed on the burner became toast in about 5 seconds per side, ready for butter. Potatoes could be sliced and likewise tossed on the hot burner plate. They took longer to brown, and if left on too long, would burn to a solid black. They also tended to be underdone on the inside; some might call them raw. Coal for the stoves was kept in a coal house off to the side of the back porch. It was filled with tons of coal, in the fall, from an uncle whose business was the delivery of coal. There were daily visits to the coal house to fill buckets for both the cook stove and living room stove.

The third floor of the house had no heat. There were small heat registers in the floor, over the living room coal stove, that were supposed to allow heat to rise to the bedrooms. There were two bedrooms, used by my two brothers and myself. Not nearly enough heat made it through the registers, and the upstairs bedrooms were cold most of the time. There seems to be something healthy about sleeping in a cold bedroom. There was little time wasted undressing and crawling into a bed capped with a half dozen blankets and comforters. The bed, at first, was very cold, but quickly warmed up. The colder the weather outside, the further under the covers we crawled, usually with just noses sticking out.

Again, in the morning, getting up and dressing for school, there was no fooling around. It was out of bed, dressed as quickly as possible, and downstairs to the warm kitchen for breakfast. Breakfasts were hearty, consisting of eggs, bacon, and home fries, or maybe Wheaties, the breakfast of champions. Sometimes, if it was available, we had scrapple, or pudding meat. Pudding meat is made from the leftover pork butchering parts such as kidneys and liver.

In the spring of the year, my dad liked to make dandelion greens. He browned bacon in a cast-iron frying pan to render bacon fat. To the fat he would add flour, and stir it until it was browned, but not burnt. Once browned, he added cold water to the mixture to make what we called bacon gravy. If you like the taste of bacon, you would love bacon gravy. It was great served over bread or browned potatoes with raw onions on the side; it makes my mouth water even now. Anyway, for the dandelions, he took fresh picked and washed dandelion greens from the yard and stirred them into the bacon gravy along with a little vinegar and sugar. This he then served over fried potatoes, mmm, good. I do not imagine it was too good for the heart; but it was a wonderful treat to us kids. My brothers and I were never fussy eaters, food was too hard to come by, and we relished whatever was on the menu each day.

My dad worked as a trackman for the Pennsylvania Railroad and was often laid off work for the winter. We did not have much money, but the family was together, warm, fed, and happy. Looking back today, those times were very good.

Lessons of Susquehanna River Crabs

You learn many life lessons early in life; but do not realize their value until you are old enough to put things in perspective. Searching the Susquehanna for bait as a youth, I often sought the common crayfish (crab) for bait by turning rocks in the shallows. It did not take long for me to learn to almost expect what size crayfish to find, by the size of the rock being turned. The larger the rock being turned; the bigger the crayfish expected to be living underneath. I think that it was like a pecking order with crayfish, the most dominant, nastiest crayfish gets the big rock. I remember, when in my teens, turning a huge bolder that housed a crayfish that was a full five inches long—so big that I was afraid to try grabbing him. In thinking about this now, I believe that one could apply this same logic to humanity; you find the biggest crabs (dominant people) living in the biggest houses—think about it.

Ice Out Time

Being young in the 1950s with so much energy (I miss that energy!) only so much sitting in front of a TV could be tolerated. With my best friend living just next door, there was always some activity to get involved in. We had very little regimentation; so long as we were home at meal time, we were pretty much on our own. There was a whole world to explore. As it turned out, we lived on the wrong side of the tracks in our little railroad town, although it took me years to find that out. At a young age, prejudices are not a priority—too much fun to be had. The railroad tracks ran between the larger main part of town and the river; my house was between the tracks and the wide shallow Susquehanna River. Sometimes, the river threatened to flow through the house, but it was just accepted as a part of life.

Winters during this era were cold and snowy, and the Susquehanna River usually froze over from shore to shore. This was a progressive process as winter deepened and temperatures dropped. One day, there were slush flows as though there was a giant ice maker someplace upstream, churning out its frigid product by the endless ton. Shores would progressively freeze outward as the slush clung to the ice forming in the shallows, extending the thickening of the shelf. Then another day, the river would appear to stand still, covered with a sparkling conglomeration of slushy floes. It looked like the top of a mountain of ice cubes, rough like giant coarse sandpaper. It would look this way until a rain which froze smooth, or a snow which covered the sandpaper appearance. Once frozen, life on the river seemed to stop, although through breaks and channels that opened, it was apparent that aquatic currents and myriads of lives that it supports continued in an unseen world.

As the icy hold of winter ebbed and days lengthened and warmed, usually late February or early March, repeated rains obviously rotted the ice pack. Instead of sparkling white, it developed a sickly yellowish tint. Then one day, after a particularly heavy rainstorm, usually a nor'easter, when the winds shifted to the west and howled as they do in March, the ice would give way. For some reason, this usually seemed to happen during the night. It began with a series of snapping noises as cracks developed in the larger ice floes. Soon, the entire river churned from shore to shore as the ice flowed, like a giant conveyer belt, on its way to the Chesapeake Bay and beyond. Not all the ice was in a hurry to reach the bay, however; much was pushed onto the shores and piled to as much as twenty feet high. Smaller shoreline trees, such as the paper birches, were bent and pushed to the ground to wait for their icy load to melt. For this reason, these smaller trees never grow straight, they always point the way to the sea. Larger trees such as the maples, oaks, and poplars stood like pillars and attempted to deflect the floes with their stout trunks. The bark on the upriver sides of these trees is always scarred from the perennial battles for dignity. Occasionally, one of these stout trees, perhaps a century old, was overwhelmed by the force and weight of the ice and pulled by its roots from its tenacious grip on the river's shore.

Our house sat on the side of a hill which was the ancient banks of the river valley, sloping down to our flat backyard which was also the river's primary flood plain. We had a back porch, about fifteen feet above the lower yard, that was a wonderful place to play and watch the river on its endless journey. Usually, this wide, shallow river was well-behaved, and stayed within its shores, never approaching the hill and house. Ice breakup time was an exception. I was always fascinated by the process and watched it from the safety of the back porch.

In years when the ice was exceptionally thick, three to four feet in places, ice jams were common. Someplace downstream—at bridges, I thought most likely—the ice would wedge, and back up the whole process like a drain plug. The river was shallow, but a mile wide. It drains much of Pennsylvania and southern New York and carries a great deal of water; with it plugged, water backs up in a hurry. It was awe inspiring, and very scary, to stand on the back porch and watch the water and ice levels fluctuate by the second. In a bad jam, the level of the whole river rose as I watched, just like pouring water into a glass. As the water and ice would approach the pillars that the porch stood on, I worried about my personal safety, as well as my world.

As the jams broke the water level dropped, sometimes faster than it rose, but it left the ice it floated behind. When the breakup was done, and the river lowered to a more stable level, the ice floes aground in the backyard became a wonderful world for us youngsters to explore. There were ice mountains to climb, and ice caves to explore. Thinking now, it was probably a dangerous place to be playing, one could drop through a hole between monster blocks of ice with no easy way of climbing out. Amazingly, through all the chaos and violence of ice-out, I never found

Author's backyard, ca. 1959

any dead fish caught in the maelstrom. Apparently, they were safe on the bottom of the river in depressions and deeper channels and rode out the process without incident. I wondered how the breakup might have looked from their perspective, looking up as the icy blanket was pulled to-and-fro, and thrown off.

It took weeks for the ice mountains to melt, drip by drip, as the sun's strength grew and the days warmed. As the ice lay exposed to the sun and warmed, it seemed to rot. A heavy blow from a shovel would shatter a berg into a million slivers of ice. Sometimes, heavy rains rose the river to a level where it floated the ice away long before it had a chance to melt. Within the month, the ice would be gone entirely, and the winter put behind, as a new season blossomed.

Susquehanna River Fishing Buddies

In the early 1970s, I was befriended by a guy who was heavily into fly-fishing; and he got me interested in the sport. We were great fishing buddies until he passed away some time ago. He taught me fly-fishing for trout, and I introduced him to the smallmouth bass of the Susquehanna River.

When fishing the river, he insisted on wearing chest-high waders rather than wading wet with sneakers as I always did. We were fishing a stretch near my home one day, rather deep and swift. I showed him a spot where he could wade down the river and fish to deeper water on either side. What I did not tell him was that there was deep water at the end of this little ridge, and it would be too swift for him to wade back upstream. He got to the end of the ridge, saw that the water was getting deeper, and tried to turn and wade back; he could not and went backwards over his head. The deep water was only a few feet until it shallowed, and he was right back on solid footing and was okay. I knew that this was going to happen; I watched him go under and howled. My friend was not happy with me, but he got over it quickly because the fishing was so good. The moral is, always be wary of advice from a friend; what are that friend's true motives?

A Cold Dip in the River

When I was about 10 years old, I witnessed firsthand one good reason to stay away from the frozen river. It was during the mid '50s, and I was sick with a cold, flu, grippe, mumps, measles, chicken pox; or one of those childhood diseases that I always seemed to be suffering from. By the way; I was often diagnosed with "the Grippe," which was a fever with aches and pains. I have not heard that term since my childhood, was it the flu or what?

Anyway, my father was laid off work from the railroad, a common occurrence for a trackman each winter, and he was home. He and my mother decided to make homemade ice cream to sooth my throat and as a treat for the family. One of the benefits from living next to a frozen river was that there was no shortage of ice for making hand-turned ice cream. My dad bundled up and headed for the river with an ax and burlap bag.

The idea was to chop several large blocks of ice from the river and place them in the bag. The bag could then be pounded using the flat side of the ax reducing the ice to various sized ice cubes, perfect for the ice cream freezer. I was watching from the living room window as my father ventured onto the ice for twenty to twenty-five feet. I continued watching as he began chopping to get some good clean ice. I watched as the ice broke under his feet, and he went into the frigid river water up to his waist. I was still watching as he scrambled out of the water, back up on the ice, dripping wet and trudged back across the yard to the house. He came into the kitchen shivering, went directly to the warm coal stove to warm up and change clothes.

I came to the kitchen and told him that I saw everything that had happened. He asked me, "Didn't it occur to you to say anything to your mother about what happened?" Of course, it did not; I really was not aware of the danger, and besides, I was too fascinated to take my eyes from the window. Luckily, he fell into the shallows and landed on his feet. If the water had been deeper, or he had been pulled under the ice, I might have been missing a parent from that day on. The river scared me during the winter, I almost never ventured near it, except when throwing rocks, sledding, exploring or some other good reason.

Wading in Muddy Susquehanna Waters

I **grew up** along the Susquehanna River and was in, on, or under the river most every summer days when growing up. I was always afraid of one thing, even into my late teens, which was stepping where I could not see the bottom. It did not matter whether it was muddy water, bottom grasses, or nighttime, I did not feel comfortable walking where I could not see, even if I was familiar with where I was going. I think that the moral is that you should never rush in when you do not know where you are going.

A Buzzard in the House

Courtesy of Pixabay

No, this story title is not misspelled. It is not about the buzzer in the house; it is about the Buzzard in the house. The Buzzard in this case was the name of the pet parakeet I had when I was about twelve years old, during the late 1950s. My father worked for the Pennsylvania Railroad doing track maintenance, which was sharply curtailed during the winter months; and he was usually off work for several of the coldest. During this time, my mother looked for part time work to help feed the family. For several years, she worked at the local Kresge's five-and-ten-cent store. The first year that she worked there, she was assigned to manage the Pet Department. Mother enjoyed the job; she sold pet supplies as well as small pets such as turtles, fish, and parakeets. Because she did such a good job she was invited back to this job whenever Father was off work.

Parakeets were popular pets during these years, and the store received regular shipments to restock their cages. Buzzard was one of these birds. When a shipment arrived, any injured or sickly birds were discarded and only the healthy caged for sale. When Buzzard arrived, he was not active like the other birds and was determined to be sickly. Mother, being kind at heart, could not just discard these birds; she brought them home and tried to nurse them back to health. Buzzard was a great success story, within a few weeks, he was flitting around his cage, eating well, and chirping to beat the band. As I recall, we had as many as five parakeets at a time, but Buzzard was a lone bird when we had him. Buzzard was obviously very young, a light blue color with white markings around his face.

Being twelve and curious, I was taken by the constant activity and began spending time by the cage. To this point, Buzzard had not been named; I came up with it one day after watching an old western and then going to talk to the bird. My twelve-year-old humor thought it was a great name for him, so it stuck. Buzzard liked the attention and began coming to the cage bars whenever I talked. I heard someplace about training a parakeet to talk and whistle by repeating a phrase or whistle. Within a few days, Buzzard began mimicking my phrases. There was "Dirty old bird," or "Hello," or wolf whistles, or his name, "Buzzard." Once he got started, he mixed and matched as he saw fit; it might be something like "Hello dirty old Buzzard" with a whistle at the end. The more he chattered, the more time I spent with him, it was great fun.

After a short period of time, Buzzard started looking for me and came to the bars to get attention from me. One day, I decided to take him out of the cage to play with him. I carefully opened his cage door and put my hand slowly in front of him. He quickly climbed onto my finger, and I pulled him out. He took a long look around the room, looked at me, and took flight. It was a wild, although constricted, gyro to all corners of the room and back again. He would land on a window curtain rod for a second and immediately launch himself. After a short while, I held out my hand and he flew immediately to land on it. It was the beginning of the next phase of our relationship. We played every day, and I taught him new whistles and phrases. I was careful that all outside doors and windows were closed before taking him from the cage, and he would sit on my shoulder as we went from room to room.

Invariably, in the evening, the family sat in the living room watching the only TV in the house. Buzzard sat on my shoulder, or nearby, as the evening progressed. At some point, he would decide it was time to turn in, fly back to his cage, climb to his favorite perch, tuck his head and go to sleep.

The more Buzzard was out of the cage, the more interested he became in family activities. He loved to sample what his people were eating. His tastes ran from such things as bananas, oranges, even raw onions; but he especially loved potato chips and pretzels. He also acquired a taste for Pepsi Cola. If somebody had a glass of soda, he would fly to them, land on the hand holding the soda, and try to steal a sip. I made a discovery on the workings of the parakeet mind this way one day. I had an empty soda glass but with a few drops on the bottom. Buzzard landed on my hand for a taste but could not reach to the bottom, so I laid the glass on its side on the table. He alit next to it and crawled inside for his treat. After he had his fill, he would not just back out of the glass the way he went in, he turned around in the bottom of the glass and walked out. It was amazing to watch, but the bird turned his body 180 degrees every time. For a moment, his head and tail would point in the same direction, and we all laughed at his antics.

At Christmas time, I would set up a platform and my Lionel trains. Buzzard sat on my shoulder as I ran my trains around the oval set, cocking his head to get a better look. One day, I decided that maybe Buzzard would like a train ride, so I stopped the train and sat him on top of the engine. I started moving the train slowly and watched his reaction. At first, he had trouble maintaining his footing, but soon learned how to grasp a molded protrusion from the top of the engine. After several trips around the track, I slowly increased the speed. Buzzard loved it and thereafter would fly to his perch on the engine whenever I ran the train; it was his spot.

Today, I am amazed at how smart Buzzard was, and how unaware I was of the uniqueness of that intelligence. I found that I could direct Buzzard to fly to specific people. With him perched on my shoulder, where he always was, I would pick a person in the room, point at them, look at Buzzard, and say, "Buzzard, go kill." Buzzard looked at where I was pointing, marched down my arm and flew to the person selected. Of course, he did not kill them, just walked up their arm to their face and gave them a parakeet kiss. I then signaled "return" by motioning with my pointing finger, and he flew back to my shoulder and did his welcoming dance.

We had Buzzard for several years, but as with all creatures, he grew old, his feathers thinned, and he could not fly as well or often. Still, he enjoyed our company and chattered all day long from his perch. One day, he was quiet and sat on his perch, not eating, or moving, noticeably ill. This continued for several days and each day he grew weaker. We covered his cage with a towel at night to protect him from drafts, and on his last day, when I uncovered him, he looked at me and spewed all his favorite words and chirps while bobbing his head, apparently glad to see me. I went to breakfast but when I came back, he was gone. I am convinced that he hung on that last night just so he could greet his family one more time. It was a very sad day in the household as we laid him to rest. Today, I have come to the realization that Buzzard's time with the family instilled in me a love and compassion for all life in this world.

Susquehanna River Potholes

Courtesy of Pixabay

If you spend as much time on the Susquehanna River as I did when I was young, you cannot help noticing the odd potholes on some bedrock formations. These holes are usually perfectly round, and may be as much as a foot deep, as though they were drilled. If you reach to the bottom, you will find one, or several, pebbles lying innocently. Believe it or not, it is these pebbles that drilled the pothole. The activity occurs during higher waters, when the pothole is under water. River currents swirl into the hole, and the pebbles roll around and around at the bottom, wearing down the bedrock like sandpaper. It may take thousands of years for a pothole to form, but as they say, Old Man River keeps rolling along, flood and ebb. The moral is that it is amazing what can be accomplished with perseverance, so keep at it.

Home Delivery

The 1950s were a transitional period in American retailing. The first malls were being built in the fast-growing suburbs, while the numbers of small-town stores were declining. During this time, my town had four grocery stores, two hardware stores, two building supply dealers, two butcher shops, a five-and-ten-cent store, an appliance store, three garage/gas stations, and two soda fountains. Today, these are all gone; the nearest groceries are six miles from town. With the Second World War and the Korean War recently ended, young soldiers were returning home full of ambition. This influx of young Americans, full of self-confidence, was anxious to get on with their lives. They were settling down, getting married, having children (the baby boom), building homes, and moving to the suburbs to live the good life that they fought so hard to protect. This migration from the farms and cities spawned suburbia and the strip malls that went with it.

During the 1950s, before the transition was complete, home delivery of products was still common. Various vendors worked their routes on a periodic basis, bringing their goods and services right to your door. I remember that early in the decade, before electric refrigeration was common, ice delivery trucks were still making their rounds, delivering large blocks of ice from the then-common ice houses. Ice usually came in either 50 or 100 pound blocks that the delivery man pulled off the back of the truck with tongs. The ice block, in the shape of a huge ice cube, was crystal clear, with rounded corners and edges from the slight melting taking place as it traveled. It slid out of the truck easily on the wet wooden floor worn smooth from years of polishing by icy cargo. Most small towns had an ice house, usually related to farm supplies. This was the same place where local farmers took their apple harvest to have cider made from their crop. We had an electric refrigerator but regularly bought ice in the summertime. We had an old, galvanized-steel tub that my dad placed the ice block in. He then took an ice pick to the block to reduce it to a tub full of large ice chunks. When the block was suitably reduced, he would add a large ripe watermelon and cantaloupes to the ice to cool. We kids expanded on the fun by chasing each other around with ice cubes from the tub. On the hottest days, we filled our water pistols with the ice-cold water. Getting shot with a stream of icy water on a sweltering day will cool you off in a hurry!

Other deliveries were also available on a regular basis. In my small town, people did not own forty pairs of shoes. They had maybe two or three pairs, two pairs of work shoes and one pair of dress shoes, and took care of them, as shoes were expensive. There was a traveling shoe cobbler who replaced worn soles and heels. There was also a tinker who repaired small electrical or mechanical appliances. The Blair products salesman peddled cans of spices, mixes, and other staple products for the kitchen.

The milk man, of course, made daily rounds, picking up empty bottles from our insulated milk box on the front porch and leaving fresh milk for the day. You had to shake the milk before using it; because milk was not homogenized in those days, the cream floated to the top. Bread delivery was usually twice a week. The delivery man came to the door with a tray of breads, rolls and pastries for mom to choose from. The bread was always the freshest, having just been baked the night before. I can still taste those cinnamon rolls that just melted in the mouth.

My favorite home delivery vendor worked only during the warmer months of the year. Every afternoon, between 3 and 4 p.m., the soft sound of ringing bells would waft through the neighborhood. It was the ice cream truck, driving slowly up the street. As the musical bells' sound entered the house through the open windows, we kids dropped whatever we were doing and headed to the street. After frequent stops, the small truck stopped in front of us and the driver took our orders. Popsicles cost a nickel, ice cream bars and sandwiches cost a dime, very reasonable. We took our frozen treats and retired to the shady, cool back porch to enjoy them; it was summertime and the living was easy!

Susquehanna Valley and Railroads

As you travel the Susquehanna River valley, you cannot help but notice that the river is often paralleled by railroad tracks. This is no accident, for when the railroads were being built for the push west, they were routed along the course of least resistance, the natural gradient already in place, the river valleys. It was faster to lay track on a course that was already mostly graded, even if it was sometimes further than a direct route. The lesson is that sometimes it is better to build on something already in existence than blazing a new course to your destiny.

Making Ice Cream

Making your own ice cream is a fun event. It brings the whole family together; first, making it, then the best part, eating it. I can still visualize the process. Dad would head for the river for some fresh ice. Mom would make the ice cream mix, a combination of milk, sugar, eggs, and vanilla flavoring. Fruits such as peaches or strawberries or nuts could be added to the mixture for flavored treats. The mixture was poured into the churn canister, which fit in the middle of the ice cream maker. The top and hand crank were locked down to hold the canister in place. Around the canister was a fiberglass tub which was carefully layered with ice cubes and generous portions of rock salt. Then the adventure began.

The younger members of the family started cranking the handle to mix and churn the mixture inside the canister while the ice and salt worked their miracle. It was easier churning at first, so youngsters started. I did not know how it worked then, but the salt melts the ice, making it colder than the freezing point of water (32 degrees Fahrenheit). The cold is picked up by the metal canister and transferred inside to the ice cream mixture. The ice cream freezes from the outside in. The mixture freezes against the side of the canister, and is scraped off as it is churned, so it must be continually turned and stirred. As it begins to freeze, the constant churning also works air bubbles into the mixture, making it lighter and creamier. Freezing makes the mixture thicker and harder to churn. By the time the ice cream is ready, it is real work to turn the handle. Lastly, you leave the freezer sit for a few minutes to harden, that is, if you have any patience left. Finally, you remove the top and crank mechanism, remove the canister from the ice/salt mixture, open it, and feast until you get a headache, good stuff.

Susquehanna River Grass Patch Ecosystem

The next time you are driving along the Susquehanna River during the summer, pay attention to the beautiful grass patches growing around the river's rocks, islands, and in the shallows. These grass patches may appear to be simple and unimportant, but in fact, they are critical to the river, its character and life forms. The grass patches themselves are like a jungle, home to insects such as coffee bugs, stone flies, caddis flies, damselflies, and dragonflies. On the bottom are leaches, crayfish, tadpoles, and frogs. The outside edge of the grass patch is patrolled by small bass, shiners, chubs, and suckers searching for wayward insects. These fish seek cover in the edges for protection from larger predator fish. The grass patch and the slack water below filter silt and other particles from the moving water. Because the grass patch slows a section of river, the water runs faster around it, creating riffles oxygenizing and cooling the water, improving the flow. The riffles are the home to other insects, mayflies, caddis flies, and hellgrammites, smaller bass, and another feeding zone for larger fish. Interspersed grass patches have the effect of mixing and turning the flowing river water as it flows past, cooling and aerating the river. A simple Susquehanna River grass patch is an ecosystem unto its own. So, you see, even as a small grass patch is an important part of the whole river, so are small parts of your character and makeup an important part of you, do not overlook anything.

Tough Times

Courtesy of Pixabay

Oakley, my Australian cattle dog, was used to rising early because of our work schedules, so on Sunday, I went out to the backyard with him around 6:30 a.m. when it was just getting light. It was cold and very windy, but from one of the azalea bushes, I heard the soft song of a sparrow. I have noticed and heard the birds more each day as we irrevocably approach spring; it is frigid and cold now, but warmer days will come. The birds know this, so sing their cheery greeting each day to herald its coming. I grew up with an interest in birds, feeding them every winter from a feeder near windows in the old house where I lived. During the winters with deep snows in the late '50s and early '60s, I sat and watched them for hours. In the depth of winter, the cardinals, juncos, sparrows, and chickadees made regular visits, to the point that I could recognize individual birds. When not feeding, they gathered in the nearby rose bushes and lilac trees where they preened their colorful plumage. What amazed me then, and amazes me to this day, is how a small bird weighing just ounces can survive through the rigors of winter. They sing their song of life because they know that the tough times of winter will pass and spring will come again. I think of them when I am in a stressful situation; that my hard times will pass, and good times will come.

The Pennsylvania Railroad

Courtesy of Pixabay

A **large part** of my family's life when I was growing up was the Pennsylvania Railroad. The railroad was the reason that I grew up in the little town where I did. My parents originally moved to town soon after they were married, because my father got a job working for the Pennsylvania Railroad at their Enola Yards. This was just after World War II when the railroad was bustling with freight and passengers. Shortly thereafter, there were cutbacks at the Enola Yards and dad transferred to the right of way maintenance group supporting the Central Division of the Pennsylvania Railroad. The Central Division maintained the tracks from just north of Marysville on west to the Altoona yards.

Dad was a physical laborer and worked very hard during his life. His job was as part of a crew working on maintaining the railroad tracks. This consisted of replacing railroad ties, rails, and the ballast that holds them in place. The railroad provided what they called camp trains which travelled from town to town throughout the district where maintenance work needed done. The camp train was parked on a siding for that purpose, usually found at the edge of the town. When the crew was working away from home, too far to drive daily, dad spent the week living on the camp train, coming home on the weekends. As I said, it was hard work, but Dad thought of the Pennsylvania Railroad as his railroad and was heartbroken when they merged with the New York Central to become the Penn Central Railroad. When he came home from work, he was filthy black with railroad dirt. During summers, he took a bar of soap and headed for the swimming hole in the river to clean up. I often went with him, and we would swim for a short while.

Early in the 1950s the Pennsylvania Railroad was still running steam engines from the Enola yards to points west. Sometime during the decade, they retired the steam engines and switched to diesel power, which was cleaner and more efficient. The steam engines, as I recall, were massive, noisy, dirty beasts, but I loved them. The railroad tracks were just across the street from our house, so I got to see a lot of trains during my childhood. You could see the steam and smoke from a steam engine long before it got near the house. As they passed, first you heard the chugging of the engine as it powered its way to the west. When the noise of the engine was past, there was the clickety-clack of the various rail cars as they passed over the joints between sections of rails. Railroad cars came in several types with box cars, coal cars, and ore cars being the most common. Without looking, you could almost tell which type of car was passing by the length of time and the tone of the click-clacks. Sometimes a wheel had a flat spot which made a thump each time it came to the rail. The steam engines regularly started grass fires during the dry season, as hot sparks dropped from the smoke stack on any dry grass along the tracks. As the result, the edges of the tracks were kept clean of plant growth.

Steam engines were very dirty to be near. Part of the coal that they were burning went up the smoke stack as cinders, which fell downwind of the train. If you were walking on the road next to the tracks, and the wind was blowing that way, you could expect a nice shower of back sooty cinders on your head and clothes. The cinders over time became a part of the topsoil along the tracks and in our front yard, black sooty soil that was easy to dig, but poor for growing plants.

The railroad tracks were fifty feet from my bedroom window, but nothing could put me to sleep faster than listening to the clickety-clack of a passing train. I was asleep long before the caboose rolled by. One of the neatest and scariest memories about the nearness of the railroad tracks was the train derailment that occurred right in front of our house. The tracks were elevated above the street level at this point, and several coal cars jumped the track and plunged down the retaining wall to end up on the street. One of the cars stopped just a few feet short of demolishing my father's car, which was parked on the street. It was lucky that no cars were passing or people walking at the time, or they would have been crushed. It took more than a day for railroad workers to clear the damage, during which time our street was basically closed.

The Pennsylvania Railroad also influenced the ecology of the Susquehanna River. The Central Division railroad lines followed the Susquehanna and Juniata Rivers or their tributaries for much of their route. The line was generally built just adjacent to the river system. The steam engines generated so much coal cinders that they became a part of the river bottom. The cinders were relatively light, and in high water, they washed downstream easily. Where there were deep eddies along the shore, the cinders accumulated to great depth. Many railroad ties also seemed to make their way into the river system. I do not know if they were washed from the tracks by high water or if workers disposed of old ties by dumping them in the river, but they were everywhere. Over time, the ties became water logged and sank to the bottom where, because they were treated with a preservative, they lasted just about forever. As they eventually rotted, they became the home of aquatic insects, crayfish, and minnows, so were not necessary a bad thing. They also anchored silt on the downstream side, which allowed aquatic grasses to grow, which became cover and food for small fish.

Growing Potatoes

To the rear of the little old tar paper house where I grew up, on the shores of the Susquehanna River, we kept a small garden. The soil was soft and loamy from centuries of river floods, perfect for growing vegetables to augment our table fare. As my father worked long days on the Pennsylvania Railroad, it was up to me to weed and tend to the plot. One part of the garden was devoted to growing potatoes. In the spring, we would buy a large bag of seed potatoes; cut them into pieces with an eye in each, because it is the eye that forms the potato plant. These were planted carefully in rows from one end of the plot to the other. Through the summer, the plants grew lushly above the soil surface while potatoes formed under the soil. Early in the fall was my favorite, the digging of the potatoes. My father and I started at one end of the potato patch and worked through, digging carefully around the plants with pronged forks. We lifted the clump of soil and brought it down hard upside down. The soft soil fell away, revealing the buried treasure, large fresh new potatoes. There is a life lesson in this story though, in that people that seem to be nothing but showy may have great substance hidden below, it just takes a little digging.

Confidence

During my life, I have been fortunate to have met, spent time, and talked, with a number of famous people. People such as Senator Ted Kennedy, Senator Patrick Moynihan, Henry Ford III, Benny Goodman, Howard Cosell, and others. The one point that struck me, common with all, was their confidence in their own personas. Self-confidence can carry one a long way so take a long look at yourself, know and deal with your weaknesses, but exploit your strengths, have confidence in them and yourself; it can carry you far beyond where you might imagine.

Mom and the Drunk

This story needs a couple of facts established before it can be told. First, I had two older brothers, six and seven years older than me. I guess that after two boys like them, my parents took a long time deciding if they wanted another challenge. At the time that I was eleven in 1958, my oldest brother Paul was eighteen. The second fact was that our mom was one of the sweetest and gentlest humans ever to walk the face of this earth. She was always smiling and understanding, no matter what the situation was. In 1958, when the rock and roll culture was approaching its zenith, Paul was totally into it. He had the ducktail hairdo, white T-shirt with cigarettes rolled up in a sleeve, leather jacket, and of course, his motorcycle. The motorcycle was not new, but it ran, and it was loud. The only place to park on our narrow street was on the edge of the road as close to our front yard fence as you could get. On the opposite side of the street was a stone retaining wall with the Pennsylvania Railroad tracks on top. Where cars were parked, traffic could not pass in both directions at once, somebody had to yield.

It was well known at the time that the town drunk also lived on our street. His name is not important anymore, but he was usually loud and obnoxious, even when sober, which was seldom. As I was saying, I was 11 years old at the time. It was in the fall of the year, early evening. I was watching TV after getting home from school. Suddenly, there was a loud crash from the front of the house. Everybody who was home at the time, my mother, Paul, and I rushed to the front porch to see what had happened. It seems that the town drunk had crashed his car into Paul's motorcycle and destroyed it. He was still in the car, backing up and preparing to drive away. Paul ran in front of his car and forced him to stop. Actually, in the drunk's inebriated condition, it is a wonder that he did.

Paul asked him if he had insurance, and how he was going to pay for the damage. The drunk got out of his car and replied that he was not going to do anything, and took a swing at my brother, knocking him down. At this point, mom rushed into the fray. She began pummeling the drunk with lefts and rights, just like a windmill. My mouth dropped open in disbelief. All the drunk could do was stumble back against his car crying, "No, no, madam, I'm sorry, please stop hitting me," and he sank to the ground, crying. Finally, mom abated; the drunk was beaten. He meekly got his insurance information from the car and shared it with Paul. From that day forward, he was always very polite to mom, and avoided the family like the plague.

Living by the Susquehanna

My parents, having grown up on farms, put their experience to use to make ends meet whenever possible. Our backyard, which was on the Susquehanna's flood plain, sported a large garden. The soil, with fresh deposits of sandy loam deposited each time the river flooded, was very fertile. We grew large crops of beans, lettuce, and tomatoes. Root crops such as potatoes, carrots, and radishes did exceptionally well in the soft soil. We were, however in constant battle with others who wished to share the bounty. No, it was not the neighbors or even the railroad hobos who frequently traveled the freight trains in those days. It was the local suburban wild critters who competed for the harvest. There were, of course, rabbits and ground hogs aplenty.

But there was also a mystery varmint who particularly seemed to like the tomatoes, just as they reached their peak of ripeness. Ripe tomatoes simply vanished overnight. The only clue was the paths of flattened grass leading towards the river. Eventually, the puzzle was solved; the paths were made by muskrats that lived on the river shore and dug tunnels and dens in the riverbank. Muskrats usually feed on aquatic vegetation, grasses, and sedges that grow under the water or on the banks. Apparently, they also relish the taste of fresh tomatoes and will travel a considerable distance to get to them.

I partnered with my uncle Bob for a time in the muskrat trapping business. We placed drowning sets along the shore at likely locations in hopes of catching the furry little critters. A prime pelt was worth about $5.00 at the time, a lot of money to me. A drowning set was a leg hold trap placed just off shore so that the chain did not allow a trapped animal to reach dry land. When a muskrat was caught in it, the weight pulled him under water until he drowned, hence the name. Minding the traps was not too bad. I checked them at least once a day, harvesting any muskrats caught and resetting the trap. Uncle Bob came regularly to skin the pelts and take them to the fur dealer.

I learned one day why trappers used the drowning set. When checking my traps, I came across one where the muskrat was able to crawl to land. He was not a happy camper, you really do not want to mess with a mad muskrat, their little incisor teeth are razor sharp. I finally had to get a big, forked stick and push him back into the water where I held him under until he drowned. It was not a good experience; it bothered me a lot and I soon gave up on being a trapper.

We also raised chickens on our little homestead. There was a large coop in one corner of the yard with a high fenced-in area surrounding it. Raising chickens was kind of neat most of the time. Gathering eggs was one of my favorite chores. It was like treasure hunting, checking each hen's nest and stealing their bounty. We always had a rooster in the flock, so occasionally one of the hens hatched a brood of chicks. They were cute and soft when little, but needed extra care to make sure they were kept warm if there was a sudden turn to cold weather. As they grew, they became part of the flock, and eventually dinner.

There were always weasels around, looking for an easy meal. Weasels are much smaller than you would think, although they are a vicious predator, fearful of nothing. Father trapped or shot them when he could, but they were very secretive.

Speaking of roosters, there was one bird, in particular, that caused problems. I must have been about eight or nine years old at the time and fed the chickens every day. The rooster that we had at the time really did not like me. He rushed at me with his hackles up every time I entered the pen. One day, he went beyond that and attacked me, talons, and wings flailing. I think that I was more scared than hurt, and ran from the pen to the house, screaming and crying. The rooster was just protecting the pen and flock but made a big mistake when he attacked me. He was invited to the family dinner the next Sunday.

Turning a live chicken into dinner did not start out as a pretty picture. Once the meal was selected, my father caught it and took it to the chopping block underneath the back porch. He held the chicken by its feet and laid its neck across the block. One quick chop with the ax and it was all over, or so it seemed. One thing that you learn from the experience is that a headless chicken does not just lie there. The wings beat and the feet race, a headless chicken will flap and run for a long time, yuck! We then plucked the bird by grabbing hands full of feathers and yanking. Once down to the pinfeathers, we singed the bird with a hot flame to burn them off. At last, the bird was ready to stuff and roast for dinner. It is easier and a lot less gory to go to the local market for poultry these days, and probably cheaper as well.

The canning of fruits and vegetables was also an important part of the little farm on the river, helping to stretch food dollars. My mother canned green beans and tomatoes from the garden. She also visited the local fruit market to buy peaches, pears, and cherries in season. These were "cold packed" in canning jars and stored in the back cellar for use throughout the year. She especially liked canning sour cherries, which she used during the winter to make the most delicious cherry pies and something she called cherry pudding. Cherry pudding was like a very moist cake with sour cherries baked in. When served in a bowl with milk and sugar, it was to die for.

My father helped my uncle at butchering time, at his farm in the country, providing meats that Mother canned as well. One of Mother's specialties was canned pork spareribs. The ribs were cooked, then canned with broth from the cooking. When opened, the meat just fell off the ribs and melted in the mouth, delicious. For years after my mother passed on, I was still able to enjoy fruits that she had canned, as good and tasty as the day she packed them.

On Stalking Carp

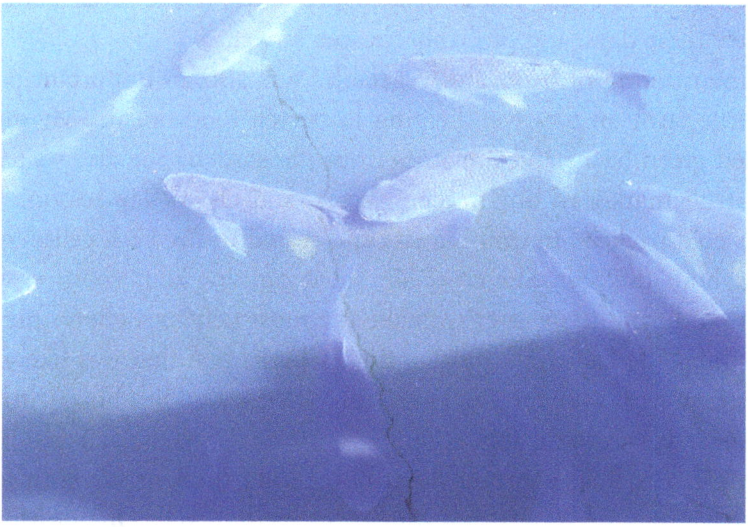

You may think that this article is misnamed, and should be "Stocking Carp," as when one plants juvenile carp in a water system, but the title is correct. This article does refer to stalking carp, as in sneaking up on them. The carp that I stalked when I was young inhabited the Susquehanna River system in Central Pennsylvania. Carp were not native to the river system but were stocked, or introduced, many years ago as a potential food source. They are a large bottom feeding fish which love to root around in muddy or grassy river bottoms. During low water periods when they do not feel exposed to predation (such as dark, foggy, overcast days), they will not hesitate to venture into shallow water to hunt food. They are easy to spot during this time because they will disturb the water surface or stir up visible mud trails as they work over an area. Watching the water surface from my backyard or porch, I would look for the telltale signs of feeding carp, and the stalk would begin.

There are two methods of stalking carp. The most challenging would be to launch my leaky wooden boat at the river shore and pole to the feeding area. I then attempted to sneak up on the feeding fish from downstream, where their vision would be blocked by the stirred mud. When close, I attempted to "bop" the carp on the head with my boat pole. The feeding carp would be two to three feet long, and the bop was never enough to cause serious physical harm. Even if it was a close miss, the carp would explode into a panic and race for deep water like a bullet. In the shallow water, the panic run looked like a torpedo leaving a sizable wake. Often the panicked carp ran into another fish nearby, and there were multiple torpedo wakes. I thought that this activity was great fun and sport and looked forward to the right days to pursue it, even if it was raining.

The second method of stalking carp was again to head to the river shore, but instead of taking the johnboat, I grabbed my trusty spinning rod on the way. I then rigged the rod with a hook and swivel, and bait with a worm or crayfish, whatever was available. It was important to have no weight on the line; the bait had to look natural. I then waded within casting range of the feeding carp and carefully cast my bait just a few feet upstream. Sometimes the fish saw the bait appear in the water column and made a beeline to it; sometimes it just picked the bait off the bottom.

In any event, I could tell that the fish had picked up the bait because my line would begin moving with it. I then set the hook and held on. Again the startled fish would take off like a torpedo, only my line was attached to it. Line peeled from my reel as it ran, and the reel's drag whirred. When the fish stopped, I tried to regain line, which sometimes initiated another run even further away. These battles were never quick. A large well-fed carp in warm water is a worthy adversary and tireless. Many times, they would break off on one of their runs or during the battle to regain line if I put too much strain while retrieving line. Other times, they continued running until my reel was almost empty; at which time I had to break them off. In any event, it was rare that I was able to land one of these fish; the advantage was always on their side. When I was lucky enough to land one, I removed my hook and sent him on his way, while I watched for another target within casting range.

My family never ate carp, because you never knew where they had been feeding, but there were some families in the neighborhood that did. I did, however, hear of one good recipe, which you may have heard.

Take a large carp, scale and gut it, and nail it to an oaken wood slab. Bake the slab and fish for two hours, remove from the oven. Throw the fish in the trash and eat the board.

To me, they were a part of my ecosystem, and I was glad that they were. I was happy that at some time in the past, somebody stocked them in the Susquehanna River so that I could stalk them.

The Old Screen Door

Courtesy of Pixabay

It is early morning, and the sun is just rising over the low ridges to the east, across the broad Susquehanna River. It is low in the sky and looms large, reflecting brilliantly from the riffles and eddies of the river below. The morning is bright and airy, already warm as they often are in the long days of midsummer. The shoreline of the river is lined with aquatic sedges, grasses, thistles, and lilies both in the shallows and on the shore. Just downstream a great blue heron is wading slowly and gracefully along the edges of the grass, looking this way and that, watching for the unaware minnow or crayfish. Just now, he freezes, cocks his head slightly, adjusts his aim and picks a careless chub that has swum within range.

Nearby on a large boulder a smaller cousin, the green heron, is also fishing, intently watching for a minnow to swim within striking distance. The blue heron with his long legs and neck is a hunter, patrolling the shallows seeking game; whereas the green heron, with shorter legs and neck, relies on the ambush, watching for prey that is unaware. A bit further from shore is the S-shaped wake of a water snake swimming upstream. Near the shore the current is slow, and the snake can travel as easily through the water as other snakes do on land. Sometimes the wake disappears as the snake dives beneath the surface seeking the minnows that he feeds on. This is my view of the world; today and every day; this is all that I can see.

You see, I am the old screen door to the back porch of a house sitting high on the river shore. My house is very old, having been built during the railroad construction boom of the 1890s. I have hung around here for a long time; my wooden frame is worn by the touch of many hands opening me to enter or leave the kitchen on the inside. Opening is easy on me; I swing freely on my trusty hinges; however, it is the closing that gives me headaches. I am attached by a spring, from my frame crossbar to the door frame, and it pulls me closed much too quickly. When opening, there is a slight creaking sound as the hinge rotates and the spring stretches; but the closure is punctuated with a loud BAM as I slap into the frame. It is this that gives me headaches from the noise and the vibration of my entire frame each time. I have had many coats of paint over the years, from white to battleship gray to the forest green coat that I am now wearing. Time means little to me, I do not know how long I have hung here, but now I hear the radio inside talking about a presidential campaign between two men named Nixon and Kennedy.

This is my view on the world; I know nothing of what is happening on the other side, the front side, the western side of the house. I believe that there is a brother screen door there, but do not know for sure. I do know that I sometimes hear a BAM from that direction and assume it is somebody letting that door slam; but I cannot say for sure. I do know that storms approach from that side of the house; I see my sky darken and then the rains and winds come. I watch the maple trees tremble at the fury but stand tall and stout, they are not afraid of any storm. As the storm passes, I see it retreating across the broad river below with torrents of rain beating the surface to a froth, then slacking off to an occasional dimple as the last drops fall.

I greatly enjoy the evenings; as the shadows lengthen and my family and world settle down. I watch nighttime spread across the river as I slowly lose sight of the distant shore, then mid river, and finally my own shore. As darkness comes, the river shore comes alive with a symphony of sound as the creatures of the night sing. In the air, I can see scores of bats flying here and there in acrobatic flight homing in on flying insects.

Why am I telling you all this, you ask? Why, because I am just hanging around, and would like to relate to you what I observe in just one day with my house and family. My house is home and shelter to three people, The Father, The Mother, and The Boy, who have been living here for some time. It is The Father who rescreened me, painted me this bright green, and rehung me with a new spring just last summer. He is a strong man, but with a tender spirit and heart, handling me with care as he refurbished me.

5:30 A.M.

I am busy watching the old man who lives next door quietly pole his wooden boat upstream for a morning of fishing, when I realize that The Father is astir in the kitchen. He works for the Pennsylvania Railroad as a trackman on the railroad's central division. The central division is comprised of all lines and spurs between the towns of Duncannon and Altoona. The Father works with a crew that maintains those tracks, mostly replacing rotted ties or reworking ballast. It is tough manual labor, and The Father's hands are hard and calloused from years of work. The Father's crew is supported by a camp train that is moved from section to section, moved into sidings while an area is worked. When the crew is working far from home, The Father will spend nights on the camp train rather than traveling back and forth. Today, the crew is working close, and The Father is commuting from home. His work day begins at 7:00 a.m., so he is up early, making breakfast and dressing for a hard day. I feel a hand on my inside frame as he quietly opens me, carrying a cup of coffee onto the porch. He then slowly closes me so as not to wake the family. The Father stands at the porch railing, sipping his coffee and taking in the beauties of the early day. For a moment, I feel an affinity with the man as we observe the same world. When he is finished with his coffee, he again gently opens and closes me behind him. I appreciate the gentle handling; it is a good beginning to the day.

6:45 A.M.

The Boy is up! Without seeing him, I know that The Boy is up. I can hear him running down the stairs to the kitchen. The Mother has told him many times not to run, but he is twelve and full of energy, so much to do, so little time to do it. As I hear him coming, I know what will happen. He will jump the last three steps and immediately turn right to shove on my frame. It is the same thing every day; the first thing he will do is go outside on the porch to survey his realm. As he passes, there is no careful closing, BAM as I slam shut. The Boy runs to the railing, he takes a long look at the river; has the level risen or fallen during the night; has the water muddied or cleared; are more rocks exposed than before. All these factors enter into his decision to go fishing or not go fishing today. The Boy likes the river low and clear, the lower and clearer the better for his fishing. In the end, it does not really matter what the river conditions are, The Boy will go fishing as he does most every day during the summer.

After checking the river, The Boy makes a survey of the other factors that will affect his plans for the day. He looks at the sky; it is azure blue with just a few fluffy clouds; just perfect for fishing or softball or exploring or whatever activity comes to mind. One thing for sure, it is a beautiful day, much too nice a day to spend indoors. Once his survey is done, desperate hunger overcomes The Boy and he heads back to the kitchen for a bowl of Rice Krispies, or apple pie, or leftover roast beef, who knows. In any event, he grasps my door handle and gives a quick tug. I fly open with a loud creak, and The Boy enters, then BAM as I slam shut again, it is going to be a busy day.

6:50 A.M.

Here comes The Boy again, BAM goes the door. He is carrying a roast chicken leg and a piece of buttered bread as he plops onto the wooden swing hung from the rafters. The swing has been my constant companion for years, although it gets to rest in the back corner during the long Pennsylvania winters. The Boy pushes on the porch floor and the swing responds, back and forth, but not fast. Just fast enough to keep The Boy content as he enjoys his unlikely breakfast. After he eats, The Boy swings for a long time; it is just wonderful to be young and alive on such a beautiful day.

7:00 A.M.

The Mother is up, I can hear her call to The Boy as she descends the stairs to the kitchen; no step jumping for her, but she does stop at the bottom of the steps to look through my screen at the sylvan view across the backyard and river shore. She is asking The Boy about his plans for the day and asks him if he would mind riding his bicycle uptown to pick up a few needed items from the Grocery Store. Of course, The Boy does not mind, this can be his first adventure of the day.

7:30 A.M.

The Boy is on his trip to the grocery store. The Mother gave him a five-dollar bill and a short list of needed items, including a box of Ivory Snow. That means that today is to be wash day and I will be busy. I saw The Boy take his bike off the side of the porch and set off on his adventure, rather, errand. The Mother and I are enjoying our time of peace together while he is gone. She is gentle and opens and closes me with care as though she realizes all that I go through and feel. Right now, she is sitting on her wooden rocker in the porch corner with a bowl of cereal and a cup of tea. When The Boy returns, she will get busy with her chores. She likes to get everything done in the morning while the day is still cool and airy. During the warm afternoons, she likes to settle in the living room with the oscillating fan watching her favorite soap opera, *Days of Our Lives*.

8:30 A.M.

The Boy is back from the grocery store; I hear him riding his bike down the side yard and bumping into the door stoop at the side of the porch. Yes, there he is; his bicycle basket full, with two paper bags of groceries and a smaller bag from the hardware store. The Boy makes regular visits to the hardware store, buying everything from fishing line to skin diving fins to spikes, using the money that he earns from his paper route. I think the store would have to close if they did not have him as a regular customer. Today he has bought a bag of ten penny nails for some purpose. I heard him yesterday, talking to the neighbor boy, Steve, about building a boat. I heard so much pounding afterwards that I think that he is building a yacht but who knows. Sometimes, boys will just pound nails for the sheer joy that the noise gives them. In any event, if it is a boat, I will be entertained as he drags it to the river and tries to make it float. It seems that it is a lot easier to build a boat than to build a boat that floats; but what do I know about boats. Anyway, The Boy is home, and his energy has not abated; BAM as he enters the house.

9:30 A.M.

The Mother has been in and out several times. Since the sun is shining brightly, she has strung her clothesline in the side yard. She uses a ringer washer and has always hung her wash outside to dry. On sunny days like today, she uses the side yard; on rainy or threatening days, she strings clotheslines on the porch. I do not like clothes hanging on the porch; it blocks my view of the river and backyard. Who wants to stare all day at a row of men's underwear, how boring?

10:00 A.M.

Since The Boy came home from the grocery store, he has been working on something underneath the back porch. I cannot see, but I hear him pounding again down there. If it is a boat, it may not float just for the sheer weight of the nails; how many can it take to hold it together? Every now and again, he makes a brief appearance, getting a glass of water, an apple or other snack; then off he goes to his project.

12:00 NOON

The clothes washing is done; it is just a matter of waiting for everything to dry, then gathering it into clothes baskets for folding and ironing. The Mother will take her time at this, the day is fair, the sun is warm; there is no hurry. The Mother has opened a can of noodle soup and has called The Boy from his pounding; ah, some relief from the noise. Here he comes running up the steps to the porch, he snaps me open and BAM, so much for quiet. They are sitting at the kitchen table talking and eating their soup with buttered bread. On the radio I can hear Arthur Godfrey playing his ukulele and singing off key.

1:00 P.M.

Lunch is over and The Mother has retreated to the living room to watch her soap operas and rest before beginning dinner preparations. Better yet, I just saw The Boy march across the backyard in shorts and sneakers carrying his old spinning rod; he is going fishing; he will not be back for at least 15 minutes. It's time for me to take a rest, I have been pulled one way or another all morning, it is enough to wear out my hinges, but I am tough, I can take it. Ah, the peace, the quiet.

2:45 P.M.

Fishing must have been good; here comes The Boy, dripping from head to toe, carrying a stringer of fish. He has two large sunfish and a rock bass to match. I have heard The Mother say that these are her favorites for eating, not strong tasting but meaty. He leaves the fish lay in the lower yard while he runs up the steps and BAM, runs into the house. I no sooner settle into the frame when, whoosh, BAM he is back out, carrying the butcher knife, and down the steps, more carefully this time. He quickly cleans the fish, buries the scraps around the flower bed and comes back up the steps. It is time to do his paper route, so he hands the cleaned fish to The Mother and off he goes on his bicycle. He has been doing this route since he was nine and has never missed a day. Every day by 3:00 p.m. he is on his way to deliver papers. The Mother will add today's fresh catch to yesterday's; and serve fried fish and fried potatoes for dinner one night. It is a tasty inexpensive meal that everybody loves.

3:30 P.M.

The Father is home from a long hot day re-ballasting track along the main line of the Pennsylvania Railroad. Ballast is the stone that forms the base and support for the cross ties that support the heavy steel rails. Without the ballast, the ties and the rails are prone to shift out of position, resulting in the derailment of passing trains. The Father is dirty; no, The Father is filthy and sweaty from a hard day's work. As it is summer and very warm, The Father takes a bar of soap and heads for the river and the swimming hole not far from shore. On a day like this, there is nothing better than bathing while swimming and enjoying the cool massaging waters of the river. As he is crossing the yard, The Boy returns, having delivered his papers. He sees The Father walking to the river and wants to join him, so he rushes into the house, BAM, and returns a few minutes later in his swimming trunks, BAM. They make quite a pair walking side by side, The Father, not tall but muscular and darkly tanned from working outside. Alongside is the scrawny kid, The Boy who has not yet experienced a growth spurt. They are talking about fishing, the river, and baseball, of course.

5:30 P.M.

Dinner is underway inside the kitchen. I hear the family talking quietly as they are eating their meal of roast beef, mashed potatoes, and corn on the cob. There is a huge watermelon sitting in a tub on the porch in front of me, surrounded and covered by chipped ice from the Ice Man's truck this morning. The Boy is relating that his boat is almost built; that he did not know how to curve the bow, so it looks a lot like a long narrow wooden box; but he is sure it will float if he covers the bottom with the three gallons of tar that he bought from the hardware store last week. He is asking The Father for help dragging it to the river when he is done, and that he still has nails to drive, oh no. There's laughter at the mention of more nails and pounding, but it's okay, there is no malice intended.

6:00 P.M.

Dinner is over; the watermelon has been carved and enjoyed. The Boy loves to eat watermelon on the porch because he can spit his seeds from the porch railing into the yard below. It is a game with him, almost better than enjoying the watermelon, to see how far he can spit the seeds, one by one. The day is beginning to quiet down. The Father retires to take a nap, recouping his energy from a hard day of physical labor. The Mother is in the kitchen, washing dishes, cleaning the table, and sweeping the floor and porch deck.

This is a magical time for The Boy; it is back to the river with his spinning rod. He is going to fish, but that's only part of the adventure for him. The Boy is very much in tune with this environment and loves to investigate the elements comprising its ecosystem. He explores the shoreline with its grasses and sedges; home to minnows, water spiders, frogs, tadpoles, leaches, and small crayfish. These shelters provide haven from the aquatic predators stalking the waters, just a few feet off shore. The shallow, faster waters that flow between two small islands off shore are home to the chubs, shiners, suckers, and small bass, looking for food in the fast moving water.

Turning rocks in these waters, The Boy is fascinated by the life on the underside: caddis flies, mayflies, stone flies, hellgrammites, and aquatic worms abound, all food for the fish waiting nearby. The air above the shallows is abuzz with damselflies, dragonflies, red-winged blackbirds, and swallows, all in their own environmental niche. The seaweed undulating in the slightly deeper waters provide shelter for juvenile fish, once they leave the shallows. The Boy likes to take a screen and push it through this seaweed to examine the life within. He is fascinated by the miniature smallmouth bass, rock bass, sunfish, and catfish to be found hiding within the grasses. As will happen, time passes, all the activity, the warm sun, and cooling water finally tire The Boy and he heads home, content, and relaxed.

8:00 P.M.

This summer day is coming to its end. There are long shadows on the lawn as the sun sets slowly on the other side of the house, behind a mountain that I have never seen. The family has gathered on my porch to share this quiet time, reflecting on the day, and enjoying the cool of the evening. The Mother is on her favorite rocker, rocking gently. The Father is in the matching chair alongside, his head resting on the padded back. The Boy is on the swing, swinging gently as he works to respool his favorite spinning reel with new line from the hardware store.

Across the backyard and the river beyond, nature is settling down for the night. Along the shoreline, frogs and toads are singing their love songs. The catbird is in the lilac tree, singing his heart out with his repertoire of songs which seems almost endless. The robin sits on its nest in the maple tree chirping softly to its mate nearby. In the air, the swallows are gyrating to-and-fro, picking mosquitoes and other insects in mid-flight. In the distance, a killdeer is singing its two-note song, "kill-deer." As the evening progress and darkness comes, the birds quiet until only the occasional chirp is heard. At some point, my family decides that it is time to retire for the night. The Boy is the last to enter the house. He closes me ever so gently; it has been a wonderful day.

The Boy Runs Away

The following is a true story. It is a Friday evening, and The Boy is upset with his parents, more upset than he has ever been, not in his entire thirteen years of life. As he climbs the stairs to his bedroom, he is fighting back tears; but he is also hatching a plan; a plan to make them feel sorry for hurting his feelings.

As The Boy lies in bed, he is thinking the whole thing through. Tomorrow is Saturday and his parents will be slow to rise. The Boy, on the other hand will set his alarm and rise with the sun, he will pack a bag with clothes, underwear, shorts, shirts, socks, and such. The bag will not hold much but will hold enough clothes to allow The Boy to establish a camp, a runaway's camp on one of the low islands on the far side of the Susquehanna River. The plan is complete; The Boy will bring his clothes, along with blankets, pillows, matches, some food, his fishing gear, and his worn pup tent to his old wooden rowboat and run away (or rather row away) to live on one of the low uninhabited islands on the far side of the river.

The Boy has visited these islands only once or twice; they are two thirds of the way across the river from his home and are near the deep channel that runs close to the eastern shore. They are gravel bars and low rising, only three to four feet above the current low water level. The shallow shorelines are grown up with grasses and reeds, high enough to hide his boat from easy view. The islands themselves, from the gravely shorelines, rise to low sand hills with stunted water birch trees that will offer shelter from the wind. The islands' low height means that they are not habitable year around—they flood and are under water much of the year—however, they are habitable for a short period of time, especially during the summer, and at least until his parents feel sorry for their transgressions.

So, early in the morning, The Boy is busy. The first thing is to write a note, "I am running away from home forever, don't look for me, good-bye," and leave it on the kitchen counter. He then makes multiple trips from the house to his row boat. The first thing is to bail the boat of the river water that leaked through its worn hull overnight. Then it is the careful arrangement of his clothing and supplies so that nothing will get wet as more water leaks in. The last items to be loaded is his fishing rod and tackle box, for once he has eaten the huge box of sandwiches, snack cakes, pretzels, and sodas, he will have to live off the land (or rather water). Off he goes, riding low in the water because of all he is carrying, but The Boy is on the way to his new home on the river. As he rows, he is munching on a sandwich for energy and trying to think of a name for his new home, maybe "Islandia."

It is a gorgeous day, not too hot, but warm. The sun is now well up and The Boy is only part way to his new island home, Islandia. The islands are almost directly across the river from his home, so The Boy's rowing is mostly quartering across the current, not too strenuous but time consuming. The Boy is hungry again, and now thirsty also, so he breaks out another sandwich, some snacks, and a soda; these all taste good to a boy on his way to freedom. As he rows, he comes upon a huge boulder with a deep hole on the downstream side. The Boy has never seen this hole before, so decides to stop for a break, to fish and maybe take a swim. The fishing is not good, but the hole makes a great place to swim; there is a side rock perfect for diving and the water is unusually calm and clear. The Boy tarries here for a long time; after all, he is free to do what he wants, when he wants to do it. After swimming, The Boy lies on the boulder to dry and rest and soon dozes off. When he awakes, it is late morning, and he still has a lot of rowing to do to get to his new home, Islandia.

On he rows. After the fishing and swim, he is hungry and thirsty again, so dips into his supply box for some refreshment and finds that things are running low. Nevertheless, he takes another sandwich, some more snacks and a drink, and travels on. As he has been crossing the Susquehanna, he notices that the water itself has changed as he travels. On the western shore, the water had a green tint and is constantly slightly murky. He reasoned that this was water from the Juniata River, which enters less than ten miles upstream. The middle portion of the river is noticeably clearer but not entirely so. This water is from the west branch of the Susquehanna which merges with the north branch well upstream at Sunbury. The easternmost waters, where he rows now, comes from the north branch of the river and is the clearest, with black stained rocks on the bottom. The staining comes from coal that was mined upstream many years ago. Much of it made its way into nearby small streams and worked its way downstream to the river, leaving the black stains behind. This all leads to The Boy's thoughts about the differences in the river's waters as he reaches Islandia.

It is now late afternoon, and The Boy pulls his boat well up on the shore through the surrounding grasses. The Boy has climbed to the highest point on the island, a short stroll actually, and surveys his realm, Islandia. It is not much, not nearly as inviting as in The Boy's dreams for revenge the previous night. There are a few scrawny trees, bent low from yearly ice floes; the sand is more pebbles (well OK, rocks), and there is no good place to pitch his pup tent. On top of it all, it looks like rain is coming. The waters around and near Islandia do not look good for fishing, they are too shallow and fast with no deep pockets to hold fish. The Boy sits on a rock (his throne?) and thinks for a moment. *He's been gone all day*, surely his parents have found the note and learned their lesson by now, *Maybe it is time to head home? There's just enough food left.*

The Boy pulls his boat to shore just as the sun sets behind the mountain to the west of town and begins lugging his gear and supplies back across the yard to the house. After everything is dumped in a corner of the porch (for now) he enters the house to find his parents in the kitchen with dinner just prepared and ready to serve. By this time, The Boy is feeling a little embarrassed by the whole thing, maybe he overreacted the night before and his parents were right, and he regrets writing the note.

The Boy's father says, "Hello son, we saw the boat gone this morning and figured you'd gone fishing. We didn't expect you to be gone all day; we wish you would have left a note."

With that, The Boy notices that his note had fallen to the side of the kitchen counter. He picks it up and replies, "Sorry Dad, I did write a note, it fell to the side here." He crumples it and throws it in the trash. It was a wonderful dinner, roast chicken, The Boy's favorite, and he goes to bed early, dead tired, but satisfied with his life.

The Flight of the Dragonfly

Courtesy of Pixabay

It is early morning, and the reeds standing in the Susquehanna shallows are clothed in mists wafting softly from the warmer deeper waters of the river. The dragonfly is quietly clinging to the reed where he has spent the night; it will be too cool for him to stretch his wings and fly for some time. As he rests, other residents of the river shallows are astir. The birds were awake and singing their morning songs as soon as the eastern sky brightened. Now, they are on the wing, hunting slow and inattentive insects in the grasses along the shore in the cool morning air. The dragonfly, protected by his camouflage, is safe but as he watches, a beautiful and alert red-winged blackbird sits on a nearby rock watching for movement. As he continues to watch, a lethargic grasshopper reveals itself on the shore and is quickly picked off by the bird, which is soon back to her raucous nestling brood with her prize. Things are quiet for a moment, too quiet, when the dragonfly spots another predator in the shallows. A bullfrog has been moving quietly through the grass and is now taking aim on a damselfly who has taken position too low on a reed.

The frog opens its mouth, and like a blur shoots out its tongue capturing the damselfly long before it is aware of the danger.

What appears to be an idyllic panoramic view of the Susquehanna shoreline with its sedges, reeds and grasses is really a wild jungle, but on a smaller scale. The shallows abound with minnows, which are preyed upon by immature bass, which are in turn pursued by larger fishes; as well as birds such as the great blue and green herons, stealthy hunters who are constantly patrolling the shallows. The dragonfly is part of this jungle; he is an opportunist who lives by preying on the smaller insects of his world. He in turn is potential prey to others, such as a variety of birds, ranging from the red-winged blackbird he observed earlier, to egrets, herons, and cranes. He must also avoid the frogs and water snakes that patrol his world regularly. Even when away from the safety of the reeds, he must avoid meeting larger fish, and of course, the windshields of traffic on the nearby road.

In the early morning, the winds are calm, but as the summer sun rises, it slowly warms the shore line and the fields beyond. The warm air begins to rise and sets in motion air movements that result in the breezes and winds that our dragonfly will encounter during its flights. The breezes also help distribute the sun's warmth; even now the air among the shoreline grasses and reeds has warmed noticeably, to the point that our dragonfly flexes his wings. As he does so, a dark shadow suddenly looms over him. With his senses focused on the fate of the nearby damselfly, he has failed to detect the stealthy approach of another predator, the great blue heron. This bird is named "great" for a reason, it is one of the largest of the heron family, and a hunter of prey at the river's edge and in its shallows. It has been quietly working through the grass and reed beds where the dragonfly has spent the night, looking for just such prey. It sees the dragonfly, cocks its heady slightly to take aim and strikes. As the bird strikes, our dragonfly takes to the air in panic mode, and as the result, the Heron grasps only grass and water, and not the tasty morsel that he had expected.

The dragonfly avoided the heron's strike more by instinct than plan, as soon as he saw the looming heron, he knew he was in trouble, and the only escape route was to the air. Although the dragonfly is an insect, low on the scale of life forms on this planet, his reactions are quick, honed by millennia of such survival reactions. Dragonflies are among the fastest fliers in the insect realm, and this dragonfly soon finds himself high above the Susquehanna River, higher than he has ever been. From this height the shoreline grass and reed patch, where he was born as a nymph and lived his entire life, looks tiny and inconsequential, lost in the world that he now sees. He observes that the river is broad and long with many rocks, rapids, and grass patches as far as he can see. Each of these grass patches he senses, is a world to its own residents, prey and preyed upon. Suddenly, he realizes that at this altitude, hovering as he is, he is he may be exposed to dangers that he has never known.

Sensing this, he instinctively makes a dive for lower altitudes where he is safer and can begin the hunt for his own meal. As he dives, there is a blur as something much larger flashes past. He is on his way down and does not realize that he just avoided the dive of a hungry sparrow hawk that had spotted him hovering in the air. This beautiful little hawk was perched on a high limb of a dead shoreline tree, watching the river and shoreline, when it saw the dragonfly rise from the river and hover high in the air. It took only a moment for the hawk to decide it was prey and make its approach, diving from above.

It is now late in the morning, and the day has warmed with the intensity of the midsummer season. To most of the natural world along the river, life has slowed to endure the summer's heat; the deer are lying in the grove of pines, snoozing, yet alert. To the dragonfly, this is the time of the hunt; the insects living on and near the river are active during this time, as is the dragonfly. As the dragonfly hunts, he hovers, then quickly moves to the left or right, looking for unaware prey; mosquitoes, gnats, water spiders, even smaller grasshoppers. He has already captured and eaten two mosquitoes that he found hovering over a stagnant shallow pool cut off from the river's flow. He is on the search again, hovering very low over a deeper pool near a small river island. As he hunts, he is also hunted, for he is unaware that below the water's surface, camouflaged on the river's bottom, lies a bass who is intently watching the dragonfly above. The bass is a juvenile, intensely voracious and ready to attack anything smaller than himself. The bass measures the perceived distance to the dragonfly and launches himself up through the water column. As he breaks through the water's surface with his mouth open and ready, it becomes clear that the bass did not account for the refraction qualities of the water's surface; he misses his target, the dragonfly, by inches. As he passes, the bass tries to adjust his angle of flight so to capture the insect on his descent to the water, but it is too late; the dragonfly is gone in a whir.

On the way back to his grass and reed patch, the dragonfly spots a hapless gnat flying nearby. After a short chase, he is able to outmaneuver the gnat and captures it on the wing. The dragonfly needs this sustenance; it has been a trying day. With his lunch in hand, so to speak, the dragonfly finds his safe reed perch, eats, and rests for a time; his harrowing day is not nearly over.

The dragonfly is on the hunt again, this time patrolling a section of the shoreline that is bare and muddy. The lack of vegetation is due to the nearby muskrat den and excavations. The river muskrat is a vegetarian, digging his den into the river bank where he and his family will be secure. The muskrat's diet is comprised of water lilies, cattails, reeds, and grasses, the scraps of which litter the shore. The constant coming and going leaves this mud, just at the river's edge, moist and soft.

The soft moist mud, in turn, is just what the mud wasp has come for; it is gathering material to build its nest on the underside of the eves of the nearby shoreline home. The mud wasp is busy, its attention on gathering a full load of mud to take back to the nest; it does not detect the dragonfly's approach. Suddenly, it is in the grasp of the dragonfly, fighting a losing battle for its life. The attack is soon over, and the dragonfly has extinguished this prey, just about as large as he can handle. The mud wasp is too heavy to lift to a more secure location, so the dragonfly dines on his feast where it lies.

As he eats however, two pairs of eyes are focused on him. From the nearby maple tree in the backyard of the shoreline home where the wasp's nest was to be built, a hungry robin has taken in the scene and is preparing to launch his own attack on the victorious dragonfly. In a different direction, from the branch of a weathered river birch tree, a pert, slate-gray catbird has also seen and is making his own plans. At the same instant, both birds launch their attack from two directions for the grounded dragonfly. The birds are so intent on their prey that they do not see the other's approach. Just as they reach the insect, calmly eating on the shoreline, they collide just overhead in a flurry of feathers and fall to the ground, each in righteous indignation and sass. Of course, by the time they hit the ground, the instincts of the dragonfly have sent it zipping away to safety.

It is now late in the day; the sun has long disappeared behind the ridges to the west; the red glow of the evening is waning. The dragonfly has returned to the safety of his stout reed in the shoreline grass patch. As the noises and sounds of the daytime pass on, the songs and serenades of the evening and night take over. As darkness comes, the dragonfly sleeps. It has been a long day with dangers and rewards, just like every other day in its lifetime.

On Fishing with Women

Fishing in the company of women (and girls) adds interesting and challenging aspects to the sport. When we were first married, my wife Terry and I often rowed into the Susquehanna River for an evening of fishing. Before we met, I had a reputation as a smallmouth bass fisherman of some stature and talent, often catching large numbers of fish, some of very respectable size. After marrying, my reputation waned, and I was known as the catcher of just a few small bass. I was consistently catching bass in the seven-to-eight-inch range. It seemed that I was always casting my line into a school of small fish, but Terry said that it was the same fish following me around that I caught time after time. As my reputation failed, Terry became known as the best fisherperson in the family, with her catches increasing in size and number of fish.

The reason for my decline and her ascension was simple. Before meeting Terry, my fishing was selfish; I caught my own bait, rowed to my favorite spots, and fished the best water by myself. There was nobody with me to look out for. If there were fish to be caught, my bait was the only choice in the hole, and I prospered. With Terry, I still caught all the bait, did the rowing to my favorite water, but then things changed. Terry would not bait her own hook, so I had to do that; then because I wanted her to enjoy herself, I would point to the best spot (which I avoided so not to compete.) Then when she caught the prize bass, I had to remove it from the hook and rebait so she could catch another. The result of all this attention was that I was basically exhausted. By the time I had finished attending to her bait, fishing spot and fish removal, I was beat and had little time to fish myself. When I did, I cast to the "poorer" spot to fish and subsequently caught a piddling seven-and-a-half-inch bass (that I barely had time to land before it was time to bait her hook again).

When the fish were not biting, we often used this as a readymade excuse to head for Dairy Queen to get an ice cream cone. Sometimes, even if we caught twenty to thirty bass, we declared that if the fishing had been good, we would have caught forty to fifty; and therefore, fishing was poor that night. Dairy Queen was a regular stop on the evenings that we fished.

In addition to the wonderful tutelage that I gave Terry which made her a good fisherperson, she is just plain lucky. Most of the time, when fishing, being lucky is better than being talented; and that is what Terry is. As an example, we went on a camping trip to a small campground in the Pocono Mountains. The campground offered a pond that they touted in their brochures as a fishing lake. We decided that we would fish the lake one afternoon to catch fish for dinner. Well, the lake was very small, with a shoreline as hard as concrete from the hundreds of campers that fished it every day. It was hard to believe that a fish could even swim in it without being snagged by somebody fishing. Of course, I had to bait Terry's hook, and she cast far out into the water, at least twenty feet.

While I was getting my tackle ready, I heard her say "Larry, I'm caught on something." As I turned, she said, "Oh, wait, whatever it is, I can pull it in." She then walked back from the water and pulled the largest largemouth bass that I have ever seen out onto the beach. It was well over twenty inches in length and easily weighed over five pounds. As she hoisted it, a crowd formed, and campers started taking pictures. She was the toast of the campground, everybody wanted to know what bait she used, how far out she fished, how it felt to catch such a trophy, etc. We ate the fish for dinner, it was alright. The next morning, as we were leaving the campground, the other campers were lined up on the shore elbow to elbow fishing the spot where Terry had caught her fish.

On another occasion, we were fishing the Susquehanna for bass in an area of rocks, riffles, and grass patches. This area was always one of my favorites because there were several areas of deep water nearby that sheltered bass. The fish would leave the deep water and frequent the riffles in the evening to feed. Being a guy, and basically lazy, I would pull my aluminum rowboat part way into one of the grass patches to hold it while we fished a riffle. I had done this, baited Terry's hook and shown her the best spot, then proceeded to rig my rod to catch my tiny bass from the wrong side of the boat. Terry exclaimed that she had a fish on (already) and needed me to remove it. I looked, and she had caught a fallfish about ten inches long, which she kept in the water on her side of the boat. As I reeled my line in, there was a tremendous splash where the fallfish was waiting.

The splash was much too big for the small fallfish, which was no longer visible in the water; Terry's line now went into the water and underneath the boat. I quietly laid my rod down in the boat and told Terry that I thought something big had grabbed her fish. I asked her to slowly lift her rod tip so we could see what it was. As she lifted, a huge head came into sight at the side of the boat, holding the fallfish crosswise in its mouth. As she lowered her rod, the head slowly withdrew underneath the boat. I said to Terry, "A big musky has grabbed your fish for his dinner."

I asked her to raise the rod tip again which she did; again, the massive head appeared with the fallfish turned more lengthwise it its mouth. As she lowered the rod, I said "You can have fun with that musky, but not for long. Just wait for a few minutes, he will turn the fallfish and swallow it. You can then fight him, but he is so big, with sharp teeth, and will cut or tear the line."

Terry said, "I'm scared. Here, you fight him." She handed me the rod, and we sat quietly for a few minutes. I then lifted the rod again, and the musky was gone. Apparently, he sensed something was wrong and spit out the fallfish or sensed that "lucky" Terry was no longer holding the rod, so there was no reason to hang around. The event was not lucky for the fallfish; it was torn to shreds by the musky's sharp teeth and was quite dead.

Terry's daughter, my stepdaughter, Tia, sometimes went fishing with us. I arranged a low seat for her to sit between Terry and me in the middle of the boat. For her fishing excursions, we had bought a Mickey Mouse fishing rod. This was literally a Mickey Mouse rod, about three feet long with Mickey's picture right on the reel. Having her own rod with her favorite Disney character was a good incentive for Tia to fish. The outfit actually worked very well, able to cast her bait as well as a larger rod. The only thing was that Tia, being very young without fishing experience, often got snagged on the river bottom, bushes, rocks, whatever was around. For this reason, one evening, I rowed to a large area of open deep water below a major rapid on the river. I figured there was less chance of her becoming snagged and we could spend more time fishing.

Sometime during the evening, Terry's reel became tangled, and Tia lost interest in fishing. Terry asked Tia if she could borrow the Mickey Mouse outfit and Tia agreed. Terry cast as far as the small outfit would reach and sat it for a moment. When she picked the rod up, she told me that she was caught on something (here we go again.) She started pulling and said, "Oh, whatever it is; it's moving." Moving it was, off to the left. After a long struggle, Terry got the fish close enough to the boat to see that it was a huge carp. The carp saw us, too, and took off downriver. Tia's Mickey Mouse rod bent double. If the rod was Mickey Mouse, the fishing line was not; it was as strong as rope. I was afraid of running out of line, so said that we would have to lift the anchor and follow the fish.

I lifted the anchor and the fish started pulling us down river. Terry said again, "I'm scared."

Tia started screaming "Get it off, get it off."

Oh great, here I am in the middle of the river, with a huge carp on the end of a rope attached to a Mickey Mouse rod, with two screaming meemies. Terry tried handing me the rod, but I had to handle the boat. Eventually we caught up with the fish and I was able to release it unharmed. We made the trip to Dairy Queen that night just to calm everybody down.

On one of our fishing trips with Tia, we brought along inner tubes for the girls to float in the river when they were tired fishing. It was a warm summer day, so it did not take long for them to declare that they were tired. They took the inner tubes and waded upriver some distance and further from shore so as to not disturb my fishing. They both climbed into their tubes and started floating. We were fishing the Susquehanna which is, of course a river, and a river has a current, and the current tends to take anything floating in it downstream with it. Soon Terry and Tia were floating past me but further from shore. I waved and Terry yelled, "Larry, get us, we're floating away."

Now, I have fished this part of the river all my life and knew it well so I responded, "Stand up, the water's only a foot or so deep," which they did. So, as you can see, fishing with women is challenging but also fun and entertaining. I would not have missed these experiences for the world.

Susquehanna River Ice Jams

1960s author photo of ice jam from the backyard looking at house. (Why was I allowed to venture out on these ice floes to take this picture?

Living on the shores of the Susquehanna River gave me worlds to explore; not just a backyard but the river in all directions. The river was a constant source of life lessons, ever moving and changing. Most winters during my youth were long, cold, and snowy and as winter strengthened; the river froze over from shore to shore. With snows covering the ice, the backyard vista changed from lawn and water to an expanse of white in all directions. As spring came with warmth and rain, the river ice cracked, broke, and began moving. I often watched this happen from the safety of the raised back porch. As the ice moved, it often jammed someplace downstream, backing up the river behind it. When this happened, the ice and water that I was watching would rise dramatically, crossing the yard toward the house. At some point, the ice jam broke, and the river fell as it rushed on towards the bay. I learned from this that we should all strive to live our lives like the river, always pushing to overcome the obstacles to our goals in life.

Susquehanna River Mayflies

As you drive along the Susquehanna River and its tributaries late in the evening during the summer months, you will notice that your windshield becomes splattered with insects. Most of these insects are mayflies from the nearby stream, who have molted to their adult, winged stage and flown from the stream for their mating stage. Do not worry about the few mayflies that you have killed. Stop at any well-lit gas station on your route, and you will see thousands and thousands dancing in the bright lights. If you look closely, and you can, they are harmless; you will see all sizes and colors of these prolific insects. Each size and color that you see represents an entirely different species of the insect; in fact, there are probably more individual mayflies in the Susquehanna River system than there are humans on this Earth. If you want to be really blown away, consider that there are other aquatic insect species as well—the caddis flies, stone flies, damselflies, dragonflies, hellgrammites—the thought is truly staggering. Getting back to the mayflies, they may live one or more years on the river bottom; molt into this adult stage; then live only to mate and lay eggs, after which they die. Their entire adult life stage may last only hours, no more than several days. We should consider ourselves fortunate to have long lives to enjoy our children; and not be plastered on some windshield.

Susquehanna River Stones Unturned

I am sure that everybody has heard the phrase "leave no stone unturned," meaning to keep trying, and search everywhere. Well, this is a real-life lesson on following that motto. When I was twelve, I started my own business, the live bait business, selling night crawlers to passerby fishermen on our street along the Susquehanna River. I charged twenty-five cents per dozen, or five dozen for a dollar, and was busy during the spring and early summer months. A dollar was a lot of money, ten sodas, twenty candy bars, two spools of fishing line; it was a very good business for a young boy.

The night crawlers that I sold I caught in my backyard at night with my trusty flashlight. On a damp warm evening in April, May, and early June, I could catch as many as fifteen dozen night crawlers, easy pickings, so to speak. I went out just after full dark, in my bare feet, with a large can. I got so good that I did not even have to bend over; I could spot a worm and catch him with my toes. In mid- and late summer, night crawlers moved deeper into the soil for moisture, but the river would drop, so I hunted hellgrammites. Hellgrammites live under rocks in the river shallows and riffles; I searched every day possible, because I could sell them for three dollars a dozen, almost a fortune to me. Behind our house, in the river about thirty feet from shore, was a small island that was above water only in very low water. Between the island and shore was a favorite hellgrammite hunting spot for me. I decided that as I was turning stones, I would begin tossing them in a line between shore and the island to build a little dam. Over the years, I threw so many stones that my dam rose above the water level and gradually filled in with silt during high water. Today, fifty years later, my dam has become a little peninsula into the Susquehanna River, changing the river's flow above, around, and below it. The point is, that while you are leaving no stone unturned, you can use those stones to change the future of your life.

The Walking Maple Tree

The maple tree referred to in low water times

By the time that I was twelve or so, I knew just about everything that there was to know; really, I did, and was also mischievous. At about the same time, my brothers, who were eighteen and nineteen, were into girls. *Yuck*. My older brother was dating a young lady who had never seen the Susquehanna—or any other river for that matter. The first time that she visited, she was amazed by our backyard with maple trees and the broad river beyond; she talked about it all day. A couple of weeks later when she visited again, I told her that she had to see how the trees had moved out into the river overnight. She walked onto our back porch and was awestruck; the big maple tree was now twenty feet out in the river! She kept talking about it until I could not help it anymore and let her know that the river had risen from the rains during the week. On another occasion, I found a nest of turtle eggs near the back porch. I told this young lady that I had found a nest of rabbit eggs. She just had to see them, and went on and on again, until this time my brother told her the truth. It is a wonder that my brothers did not take me fishing and lose me, but they did not, so I lived to tell you this story of a rotten little kid.

Spring Seeps

My backyard along the Susquehanna River was full of "spring seeps" during the spring of the year. These are comprised of small springs that flow only during the wet season. There was one in particular that flowed every year, arising ten to twelve feet from the river shore. It had a steady flow that I played with; I dug around where it came up to create a miniature lake and river. It came to the surface through a single hole in the ground about two inches in diameter, sparkling clear and icy cold.

One day after playing I was parched and thirsty and, being ten or so, too lazy to go to the house for a drink. I looked at my little pond, so clear, so cold and so inviting and decided that anything so inviting must be OK to drink, so I did. I knelt over, put my mouth to the surface, and drew in a big mouth full, sat up and swallowed. As the water went down, I got an instant sore throat, burning and intense. I ran to the house, drank two glasses of milk, and worried. Of course, I did not tell anybody, duh. The sore throat lasted only a couple of hours, but I had learned my lesson, things that look clean and pure may have a dark side that you do not want to taste.

Great Leaping Bass

The 1980s were glory days for smallmouth bass fishing on the Susquehanna River. During this time, I was heavily into fly fishing and was on the river many evenings during the summer. On one particular evening, I was standing on a huge boulder, casting to the edge of another boulder with a large grass patch downstream of it. I hooked a small bass in the eight- to nine-inch class and was enjoying the spunky fight that he was giving me. All at once, he stopped resisting me and began swimming and jumping towards me with everything that he had. This was very odd behavior, and I was pulling in line as quickly as possible to keep up with him. After his second or third jump towards my rock, I saw why he was acting as he was. As he jumped, there was a huge swirl just behind, and I saw the biggest muskellunge that I had ever seen, chasing him. Well, that little bass eventually came to my boulder and jumped up on it to avoid being eaten by the musky. The musky swam right to the edge of my boulder, came to the surface as though he was thinking about jumping up also, then turned and swam away. I picked the exhausted little bass up, unhooked him, took him to the far side of the boulder, and released him in a protected cove. He just laid there on the bottom, finning slowly for a long time before swimming away. I think that the moral of this story is, that it is great to fight the good battle; but be aware, something much worse may be sneaking up behind you.

The Old Row Boat

1960s Author Photo of his father with wooden boats

Living along the Susquehanna River as a teenager, I had two old wooden rowboats that were rescued from spring floods. Actually, they were worn out, and somebody had left them on the river shore to be washed away in high water. Every spring, I spent hours caulking the cracks between the floorboards to reduce the leakage, but to little avail.

Here's an interesting story about the upright boat in the image above. I had inherited it from an older brother, Ron, when he married and moved out of the house. Soon afterwards, on a visit, he suggested that we take the boat out and fish the Susquehanna. Ron rowed upstream, while I constantly had to bail out water as the boat leaked quite badly. We decided to fish one of our favorite spots, a rock named "Whitey," a huge free-standing boulder, deep and undercut. We climbed up on the rock and began fishing with the boat tied to the side. As we fished, the boat continued to leak, slowly filling. The fishing was outstanding, smallmouth bass, rock bass, sunfish, one after another. As we fished, we decided to start throwing our catch into the now water laden boat, to sort out later. As dusk approached, we decided that we had enough fun, and to head home. Looking down at the boat, there were so many fish swimming that it was hard to see the bottom, but Ron stepped into it to begin bailing. As he did so, he tipped the balance between floating and not, and the boat disappeared below the surface, as we watched, fish of every type, free to leave confinement, did so. Ron looked up at me, still on the rock, and roared with laughter.

The Little Black Catfish

Courtesy of Pixabay

When I was a teen, exploring the Susquehanna River shore on my daily fishing expedition one day in early May, I discovered a small black catfish finning right next to the shore in an exposed muskrat tunnel. As I approached him, he swam off into deeper water but returned as soon as I backed off. I dropped a baited hook in front of him which he grabbed immediately. I pulled him from the water and looked him over. He was only eight to nine inches long, but appeared healthy, so I released him to the river. He swam back to the same spot and began finning as before. I thought that he must be ailing, so I visited the spot each day, dropping fat night crawlers for him to eat.

One day a week or so later, I returned and was surprised to find that he was not alone. Around my nine-inch catfish swam fifty or so miniature versions of him. As I approached, I was astonished, as he opened his mouth and all the tiny catfish entered, after which he closed his mouth and swam away until I backed off. He returned, opened his mouth, and the babies swam out and began feeding. I then understood that he was a male catfish guarding his mate's nest, and his own progeny. He now had no more interest in my night crawlers, only in guarding the tiny catfish. I returned every day for the next two to three weeks, and every day the tiny fish were a little bigger. It got to the point that when I approached, they could hardly fit in his mouth, and a few would have to swim away by his side. One day, they were all gone. The tiny catfish were big enough to fend for themselves and had swum away to start their own lives. I have seen this behavior in catfish only this one time in my life, but it left an impression on me. If a nine-inch catfish can devote so much care, to the point of risking its life, how much more care should we put into our lives and our own families.

Deer in the Headlights

The phrase "like a deer in the headlights" is a fact of nature; deer for some reason are mesmerized by the headlights of an oncoming car. The best way to avoid a collision is for the driver to turn off his headlights for just a second to break the spell. Usually, the deer will then bolt off the roadway to safety. Like the deer, we too are often mesmerized by the speed and complexity of our lives. Sometimes, it is good to stop for just a moment; close our eyes, and focus on the important things, our home, family, and friends.

Full Moon

Have you noticed the brilliant full moon the last couple of nights? If not, you should, because without it, you might not exist. You see, it is the interaction of the moon's gravity with the Earth's own gravity that keeps the inclination and rotation of the Earth on its axis stable. Without this planetary dance, the Earth would tend to wobble on its axis, throwing climate into chaos. The equator could suddenly shift from its present location to anywhere, even pole to pole, changing what was a tropical climate to arctic and vice versa. One of the contributing factors to the development of life on this rare planet has been its relatively stable climate over the millennia. Think of this fact in the context of your life—what keeps you on a stable axis and course through your life? If it is not readily apparent, think harder and you will realize who or what provides your anchor to life.

The Rock

Courtesy of Pixabay

This story is about a rock in the Susquehanna River behind the house where I grew up. Until my teens it, and the small pool downstream, was the site for swimming, snorkeling, diving, rafting, and fishing for my best friend and myself.

The rock is large, about the size of a kitchen table, with a flat top that in low water was barely exposed to the air.

The large rock is a conglomerate, made up of thousands of small stones pulled together and cemented by pressure. The material for the rock may once have been part of an ocean floor, buried, and bound by the weight of the millennia.

The large, conglomerate rock is ancient, perhaps billions of years old. It is out of place in the small pool where it is located, surrounded by sand, pebbles, and rocks of other types.

The large, conglomerate, ancient rock is unmovable; it has withstood thousands of years of floods and ice jams. It is large, heavy, and locked into its position in the river for eternity.

The large, conglomerate, ancient, unmovable rock is uncomfortable to sit on, the surface of small stones and bits are sharp and scratchy, but when you are young, it does not matter.

The large, conglomerate, ancient, unmovable, uncomfortable rock has a hollow pocket underneath where we stored play treasures for safe-keeping; perhaps there is treasure there to this day.

The large, conglomerate, ancient, unmovable, uncomfortable, hollow rock was the first of many river rocks that I came to know and so was named appropriately, "First Rock."

The large, conglomerate, ancient, unmovable, uncomfortable, hollow, first rock was home to many fish, sunfish, rock bass, smallmouth bass, suckers, carp, and others; it provides shelter from the currents and food aplenty.

The large, conglomerate, ancient, unmovable, uncomfortable, hollow, first, home rock to this day is my favorite, I spent almost every summer day there, splashing and enjoying life. I miss my times at that large, conglomerate, ancient, unmovable, uncomfortable, hollow, first, home, favorite rock very much.

Bricks

The common brick is made of clay mixed with sand and water, then molded into shape and heated to high temperatures, locking into its strength. The first known formed bricks date back to 7,500 BC in what is now Turkey. Bricks allowed humanity to build long-lasting fire-resistant buildings, and to this day are one of the most environmentally friendly building materials on the market. The truly amazing thing about bricks is that they are smarter than some of the bosses that I have had during my life.

Of Mice and Boys

The old house that I grew up in, on the shore of the Susquehanna, had mice; not all the time, but they tried to move in, especially in the fall with the chill and coming winter. The house was built it the 1890s during the railroad boom for workers of the Pennsylvania Railroad. It was built on the side of the hill sloping to the river with a dirt cellar, and no insulation. The mice worked their way into the cellar and then roamed the house looking for food. Having mice in your house today is a big deal, but not in the 1950s, it was a common problem in older houses. When my family heard or saw a mouse, it was my mission to catch and destroy the rodent pest. We had several mouse traps that I carefully baited and strategically placed by the cellar steps, behind the cook stove, and other likely places. Mice are most active at night, so first thing in the morning, I checked my traps and dispose of any losers from my mouse trap game. Mice do not learn from the mistakes of other mice; they keep coming back to the bait until there are none. This is a good lesson for us; learn from the mistakes of others, and do not do the same dumb things that they do.

Blood Suckers

Blood suckers is a term usually associated with financial institutions or government entities, but the term is actually applied to the feeding habits of aquatic leeches. Have you ever seen one? I am guessing not, but I had a lot of experience with blood sucking leeches in the Susquehanna River early in my life. I often came to the shore after wading, swimming, or fishing the river to find one, two, or even more leeches attached to my legs. They were attached by their mouth parts, with which they cut through the skin. They injected an anticoagulant into the wound, and sucked blood until they were bloated. They were not easy to remove; they could be pulled off but did not want to leave the feast. I learned that if I touched a hot match to their back, they would release their hold and fall off; but it was hard to keep matches dry while in the water. I often returned to the house after an outing with open wounds and fresh red blood running down my legs from the little buggers. It was ugly; but much better than the blood sucking financial institutions and government entities of today.

Rattlesnakes

At one point, I was heavily into seeking out native Pennsylvania brook trout and fishing for them. The Susquehanna is fed by a myriad of small, secluded mountain streams, many of which teem with wild native brook trout in hard-to-reach mountain valleys. On one such expedition, I was fishing slowly up a remote stream, catching many beautifully colored native trout. The stream was so hard to get to that it may not have been fished with the last fifty years. Suddenly somewhere nearby, in front of me, I heard a rattlesnake, coiled and rattling. I shifted my feet slightly, and it rattled again. I could not see it, but it must have been within ten feet of where I was standing. I looked beyond, further upstream, and saw a string of pools that I would love to have fished; but instead turned around and walked cautiously back downstream. Sometimes, it is better to turn and walk away when the risks are greater than the possible rewards.

On Throwing Knives

When I was in my earlier teens, Westerns were all the rage on TV. One day, one of them featured a man proficient in throwing knives. It made an immediate impression on me, and I decided that I, too, would become a knife thrower. The next morning, I was off to the local hardware store where I purchased several cheap low-grade hunting knives. Luckily, I was the local newspaper delivery boy and had a constant flow of spending money; not much, but enough for my needs. I came home and headed to the backyard, where the previous spring's ice breakup on the Susquehanna had partially unrooted a maple tree. It was now trimmed up, leaving only the roots and a stump on an angle away from the river, the way the ice had pushed it. So, with the top of the stump as my target—some fifteen inches across—I set out to hone my skills. At first, my aim was wild, often missing the stump entirely, but as I practiced, I improved. Other than hitting the stump, the hardest part was to have the knife rotate just enough after being thrown to strike the stump point first. Since I held the knife by the blade end, this meant that it would have to rotate just about three-quarters of the way to accomplish this. Holding the knife and throwing it, while holding the very tip, caused at least several rotations, so I kept experimenting. I found that by holding the blade further up I could cause the knife to rotate just right, about three-fourths. I practiced day after day, becoming very proficient in aim and force, until one day, somehow, the knife struck the root edge, and bounced back at me—and stuck in my leg, just above the knee. I pulled it out, blood running down my leg, and hurried into the house. I cleaned my leg, holding a wash cloth on it until it stopped bleeding, then put several bandages over the wound, and never told my parents. I carry a scar to this day, some sixty years later. After that day, I threw knives only occasionally, and very cautiously.

Annoying Birds and Bad Habits

We once had an Australian cattle dog named Oakley who was a very close friend; we took walks and had imaginary conversations. Oakley and I got to the pond for a short walk one evening, after several dreary days. As we rounded one corner, we startled four ducks who had settled near the bank for protection overnight. They flew only enough to get to mid-pond, then turned to us and chattered as though asking why we were bothering them. They were mallards, two drakes and two hens, probably paired up for mating next spring. Oakley watched, and asked me "What are those beautiful birds?"

I explained, "Those are wild ducks, mallards. They may have flown hundreds of miles, are tired, and need a place to rest."

He responded, "The only ducks I've seen were on the farm where I grew up, they were white, and I chased them for fun. Can I chase these?"

I looked at him and said, "No, we'll leave them be and go the other way. Maybe they'll stay here and raise their young; it would bring a new level of life to the pond." We continued our walk and returned to our car by the "sitting" rock. We sat, even though it was cold and damp.

We watched the crows sitting high in the trees across the field cawing back and forth and making a fuss. Oakley asked me if I wanted him to bark and scare them. I replied, "No, it would only make them worse."

Oakley then asked, "Why did God create so many annoying creatures in the world?"

I told him, "God needed a lot of practice before he created the two most perfect creatures, dog and man. Dog he named after himself by spelling his name backward; and man after; well, I do not know why he named man as man." I continued, "I do know how woman was named; it's a mistake. God originally named man's mate as woe(to)man, but it got shortened to woman." We both laughed at this; if you have never heard a dog laugh, it was hilarious.

This House is Haunted

Courtesy of Pixabay

It is the late 1950s, and I am twelve years old, lying in my upstairs bed at the back of the old house late at night. Across the hall from my bedroom door was the door to the attic. Suddenly, I hear what sounded like that door creaking open. Then came what sounded like a marble rolling across the attic floor towards the steps. Following was a *chunk* sound, as if it fell to the top step. This was followed by more rolling and *chunks* as it rolled down the entire flight. I often turned the lights on, but upon looking at the door to the attic, which was closed, and the steps beyond, nothing seemed out of the ordinary. I then went back to bed and the whole process would repeat, again and again. After my brothers left to begin their lives, I quickly moved to the front bedroom and never heard the noises again.

Quick Glimpses

Writing, like a journey, can be succinct, direct and to the point; or it can be as a tour, the route to the point being made pleasurable and fulfilling. The difference can be illustrated by first, the succinct version of an incident, "The cat is dead," versus the alternative, "The cat who has been with the family for ten years, always gentle, well behaved, a great mouser and protector of the garden, passed away quietly last evening; his soft meows will be missed by all." The beauty of the English language is that we have a choice in styles.

If you still have not discovered the meaning of life, you just have not been searching hard enough.

Modern medicine has developed cures for many maladies, but one ailment has prevailed, the common inflated ego. My mother taught me a little poem to illustrate the subject when I was in grade school that goes: "I think I'm great, I think I'm grand, I go to the movies and I hold my hand."

When you think you are in over your head, just put your feet down, you are probably in the shallow end.

When you are young, you have great energy, but no vision;
When you are old, you have acquired vision but have no energy.

The making of a plan is easy; it is the successful execution that is difficult.

Many get to the top by climbing on the backs of others;
a few will rise to the top by promoting others, they are the cream.

Being a guy, and a former smart-aleck computer analyst for most of my working career, when asked by somebody such as a sales person, if I had any questions, I would respond, "Yes, what is the population of Bolivia?" Imagine my surprise one day, when a young lady responded with the correct answer. It turned out that this lady was from Bolivia and, of course, knew. The point is that if you have a problem or question that appears to be unanswerable, keep asking, you just have not found the right person yet.

Climbing a mountain is very difficult; carrying you on my back makes it impossible.

Life is like a toboggan, so fast, so fun, so exciting, and best when shared with your soul mate.

Everybody has a warm heart, only a few are blessed with a kind and giving spirit.

What is the best way to recollect a warm or happy family moment? Go do it again, there is no limit on the good memories a mind can hold; the more memories, the more fulfilled the soul.

Every morning when you are dressing, stand before the mirror, and look yourself in your eyes. Tell yourself what you want to accomplish today, tomorrow, next week and the rest of your life. This is the path to greatness. If only somebody had told me to do this fifty years ago, what I could have accomplished with my own life.

Keep in mind as birthdays come and go, we are not getting older, we are just nearing perfection.

Talk to the seniors that you know, they have been where you have not, they have seen what you have not, they have experienced what you have not. Use them as guideposts in your life—or just go it alone and leave us alone.

A story in twenty words, pay attention: "Tweet, tweet went the birdie, Meow, meow went the kitty, Tweet, tweet went the birdie, Burp, burp went the kitty." OK, what is it about this story that is the same, and yet different? Answer, both the birdie and the kitty had tails, but their tales ended differently.

From birth, we learn to speak, we go to school and college, we start careers, raise families and all the time, it is "learn, learn, learn," drawing from the well of life. Isn't it ironic that in our old age, we tend to forget what we learned early in life, it is as though we must replenish that well of knowledge that we drew from so long ago?

Like many things in life, an outhouse is an eyesore unless you really need one.

When you're about to blow up at somebody that you care about over some situation—take a moment; pet the dog; have dinner at a good restaurant; sit on a bench by the ocean and watch the world go by; have a massage; spend a week at Disney World; take a cruise; go clothes shopping; take in a good movie; write a book about your alter ego; walk and talk with your best friend—now what was that problem?

"It's all about me (or you)." I am sure that you have heard this phrase many times; but this phrase represents the worst of humanity. One important thing that sets our species, the human species apart from others, is our ability to care for others, to have compassion for the welfare of other humans or animals. In the animal world, it really is "All about me." Did you ever hear of a rabbit bringing food to another rabbit, sick or injured; did you ever hear of a bird bringing food to another; or a fish? No, if a wolf comes across a wounded calf, kills it, and eats it. It is the ability to care for, to have compassion for other people, animals and even plants that sets us apart. So, show your humanity, your compassion, have an open and kind heart, reach out to those in trouble. By helping others, you reap the rewards—a fulfilled soul; and a better and happier life.

The universe is 14 billion years old.
The sun is 8 billion years old.
The Earth is 4 billion years old.
The Susquehanna River has flowed for 60 million years.
Modern humans first arose in Africa 200,000 years ago.
You have been billions of years in the making, so shine like a star.

You cannot climb the mountain unless you take the first step.
You cannot learn to swim unless you enter the water.
You cannot read a book unless you open the cover.
You cannot succeed in life until you make the first effort.
Decide what you want to do, and then go do it, everything is possible.

Wading the Susquehanna every summer day, I would put on my old "river" sneakers, cheap high tops, worn out with holes. Invariably, after wading for a while, small stones would work their way inside the sneaker. If I was lucky, they would end up under my toes where I could hold them still, but eventually, a large pebble would lodge under my insole and cause pain with every step. Being a lazy boy, I would deal with the pain as long as possible, before finding someplace where I could take the sneaker off and shake out the pebbles for some relief. How often in our lives do we put up with the pebbles of aggravation, small things that we could fix, but are too lazy to do so. If we could just remove one pebble every day, wading through our lives would be so much happier.

On the inside of every old man, you will find a twelve-year-old boy, just trying to get out to have fun.

As I have aged, I have developed a few health problems, aches and pains, a bit of dementia; but the important thing—I have discovered the secret for a long, prosperous, happy life which I'm going to share. It's . . . it's . . . Rats! I cannot remember, I . . . cannot . . . remember.

Living along the Susquehanna River as a teenager, I had an old wooden rowboat that was rescued from a spring flood one year. Every spring, I spent hours caulking the cracks between the floorboards so that it would not leak when in use. Although the boat was old, it served me for years of exploring and fishing the river. The same can be applied to us; if we caulk the cracks and holes in our lives, we will be able to float safely through the hard times.

Evenings and Sunsets on the Susquehanna

Perhaps my favorite time to be on the Susquehanna would be on soft warm summer evenings, with the hot sun setting behind the mountain to the northwest. This was a time of peace and tranquility on the river, the winds would settle down to gentle breezes, frogs would begin their croaking choruses and peace would settle. Cranes and egrets would be winging overhead to their nighttime retreats, while swallows would be skimming the surface of the quiet river pools. The water itself would seem to sense the coming of the nighttime calm, and settle with a low murmuring tone, restful to the soul. If the environment was calming, it was a period of heightened activity for the fishes that inhabited every deep hole; the predator fish, notably smallmouth bass would be on high alert for any unaware or careless prey that came within range. As darkness descended on the scene, rocks projecting above the water surface would take on shadowy forms resembling dragons swimming lazily upstream. I would row my old wooden, leaky boat back to its mooring spot on the shore of my backyard, tie it off, and walk towards the old house as crickets sang their song, and a myriad of bats swirled overhead.

As I walked, I would look back over my shoulder at the river, thinking of the many reflections of the Susquehanna that I had seen, and be happy and fulfilled for the day.

About the Author

Larry L Little grew up in a small Central Pennsylvania town, with the Susquehanna River flowing on one side of his home, and the main Pennsylvania Railroad freight lines on the other side. He spent his entire working career (50+ years) designing, writing, and supporting computer software systems. He spent the first 40 years working with financial (banking) systems, and the final 10 years supporting outpatient clinical computer systems for a large hospital system.

From his earliest years, he was drawn to the Susquehanna River almost daily to spend his time in, on, under or ashore of the river. His need to, "know how things work" later applied to his computer analyst profession, led him to investigate how the river worked, from its flow, to the myriads of life forms to be found.

He has had several pieces published in local magazines, but this is his first compilation in a book form. Since retiring several years ago, he has turned his attention to the writing of his memories and observations, passing on the wisdom of his experiences as a youth to a new generation.

www.ingramcontent.com/pod-product-compliance
Lightning Source LLC
Chambersburg PA
CBHW072154090426
42740CB00012B/2260
* 9 7 9 8 8 8 8 1 9 3 6 1 7 *